"Dick Allen lifts out of the Bible those traits that we can all learn, traits that make us leaders in the best sense of the word. I commend *The Genesis Principle of Leadership*."

Dr. Frank A. Brock,<br>
Center for Authentic Christian Leadership

"Dick Allen invigorates the leadership dialogue with biblical insight and practical implementation."

Dr. Gary Purdy, Senior Pastor,<br>
North Shore Fellowship, Chattanooga, Tennessee

"Dick Allen offers an insightful and challenging exploration of the biblical teaching on leadership. By grounding his understanding in the biblical notion of the *imago Dei* and exploring its implication for leadership, Professor Allen paints a unique portrait of the leader that will challenge you as you engage this thoughtful work."

Darwin Glassford, Ph.D.,<br>
Professor, Calvin Seminary

"How exciting! How refreshing! *The Genesis Principle of Leadership* is long overdue. Dick Allen's work is a must-read for those acting in key positions of leadership and those teaching leadership concepts. Clearly, it's time for you to become the leader God designed you to be. It's time for you to read this book!"

Dr. Robert J. Imhoff,<br>
President, Mid-Continent University

# The GENESIS PRINCIPLE
## of Leadership

# The GENESIS PRINCIPLE of Leadership

*Claiming & Cultivating
Your Created Capacity*

RICHARD D. ALLEN, PH.D.

TATE PUBLISHING *& Enterprises*

*The Genesis Principle of Leadership: Claiming and Cultivating Your Created Capacity*
Copyright © 2008 by Richard D. Allen, Ph.D.. All rights reserved.

This title is also available as a Tate Out Loud product. Visit www.tatepublishing.com for more information.

No part of this publication may be reproduced, stored in a retrieval system or transmitted in any way by any means, electronic, mechanical, photocopy, recording or otherwise without the prior permission of the author except as provided by USA copyright law.

Scripture quotations marked "ESV" are taken from The Holy Bible: English Standard Version, Copyright © 2001, Wheaton: Good News Publishers. Used by permission. All rights reserved

Scripture quotations marked "Msg" are taken from The Message, Copyright © 1993, 1994, 1995, 1996, 2000, 2001, 2002. Used by permission of NavPress Publishing Group. All rights reserved.

Published by Tate Publishing & Enterprises, LLC
127 E. Trade Center Terrace | Mustang, Oklahoma 73064 USA
1.888.361.9473 | www.tatepublishing.com

Tate Publishing is committed to excellence in the publishing industry. The company reflects the philosophy established by the founders, based on Psalms 68:11,
*"The Lord gave the word and great was the company of those who published it."*

Book design copyright © 2008 by Tate Publishing, LLC. All rights reserved.
*Cover design by Lindsay Behrens*
*Interior design by Jennifer L. Fisher*

Published in the United States of America

ISBN: 978-1-60462-483-0
1. Business and Economics: Leadership   2. Inspirational: Motivational
08.01.10

Sarah, I am the most esteemed among men!

Karissa and Doyle, My heart rejoices—dances—over you. You make me proud!

Sola Dei Gloria!

# Acknowledgments

It would be a colossal mistake to embark upon a project of this magnitude without expressing my profound appreciation for those men and women who encouraged me to claim and cultivate my created capacity for leadership. There are so many. Each person: teacher, professor, colleague, family member, and friend, made singular and extraordinary contributions to my full, fruitful, and fulfilling life. Each one is truly an "encounter with greatness." Each one modeled and brightly reflected the image of God in his/her life. As created leaders they were much more concerned about impacting others than material reward or public acclaim. You should be so fortunate to have one such magnificent, astonishing, and brilliant person in your life. I've had many.

At great risk I must acknowledge a few of my heroes: Loren Dietrich was much more than my high school football coach; Fred Moore would shutter to hear me describe him as "saint;" Vern Harriman pushed me toward excellence; Larry Coy always made sure I was never embarrassed by the clothes I wore to school; Leroy McGinn stood in the gap when I needed a strong male role model in my life; and, Chuck Roost, Bob Imhoff, Dale Walker, and Howard Nourse, gave me confidence to be a better husband, father, and servant. I will be grateful for the first ten billion years of eternity for these and scores of others who made "the" difference in my life. Thank you—each one!

# Table of Contents

Preface . . . . . . . . . . . . . . . . . . . . . . . . . . . . . . . . . . . . . 17
The Quest for Leadership . . . . . . . . . . . . . . . . . . . . . . . 27
Created To Lead. . . . . . . . . . . . . . . . . . . . . . . . . . . . . . 39
Leaders are Active and Purposeful. . . . . . . . . . . . . . . . . 55
Leaders are Rational. . . . . . . . . . . . . . . . . . . . . . . . . . . 67
Leaders Are Creative . . . . . . . . . . . . . . . . . . . . . . . . . . 79
Leaders Exercise Dominion . . . . . . . . . . . . . . . . . . . . . 91
Leaders Are Moral . . . . . . . . . . . . . . . . . . . . . . . . . . . 105
Leaders Are Relational. . . . . . . . . . . . . . . . . . . . . . . . 119
Leaders are Free and Responsible. . . . . . . . . . . . . . . . 137
Leaders Are Loving . . . . . . . . . . . . . . . . . . . . . . . . . . 151
Leaders are Merciful. . . . . . . . . . . . . . . . . . . . . . . . . 167
Leaders are Faithful . . . . . . . . . . . . . . . . . . . . . . . . . 183
Leaders Are Interdependent. . . . . . . . . . . . . . . . . . . . 197
Leaders Are Generous . . . . . . . . . . . . . . . . . . . . . . . . 215
The Essential Purpose of the Human Enterprise. . . . . . . 227
Endnotes . . . . . . . . . . . . . . . . . . . . . . . . . . . . . . . . 235

# Foreword

Leadership is not an option. Perhaps that's why "leadership" has become an industry, not just an intriguing subject.

There are few people who don't lead someone: a son, a daughter, a neighbor, a co-worker. A few lead many; most lead only a couple. Both by role, expectation, and interpersonal relationships, leadership is everywhere—leaders are everywhere. From many perspectives, those who have led us have formed us.

The subject of leadership has mushroomed into an industry that annually sells millions of books, prints untold numbers of magazine and journal articles, and captures thousands of seminar attendees looking for that extra-special advantage. "Experts" and "would-be experts" wax eloquent on all the skills and maneuvers a leader can employ to move people into some pre-determined, desired behavior pattern.

Possibly there's little in this human adventure that's as important as one's influence on others. The very character of life is the result of those whose influence has led us in one direction or another. So it's understandable that the subject of leadership would capture center stage in a world struggling to find significance and meaning.

For many practitioners it's simply a cause and effect dynamic. If the "leader" can create an effective causation, the effect on those to whom the causation is applied will be appropriate. The effect on the follower is directly impacted by the skill of the one exercising lead causation. Great skill—great effect; little skill—little effect.

The great gurus of business and politics and religion have been carefully and thoroughly analyzed in an attempt to uncover their leadership secrets. Most have a book they've written to share with the world the keys to their success. All have been credited with specific keys to their effectiveness—keys that, if you and I could duplicate, would launch a new measure of our own success.

But a student of leadership soon discovers a discouraging fact. The great bulk of information on the subject is simply another way of saying the same thing others have already said—or a new twist on the same motivational behavior that didn't work last time. It tickles the imagination, gives short-lived new energy to modified old patterns, but adds little to the understanding of this important phenomenon. Even when graced with a Bible verse, a pithy quote from classic literature, or a clever joke, the foundation of our understanding of leadership somehow isn't strengthened by what someone else did or said.

Dr. Richard Allen has invested his life in the teaching of management and leadership. His students, whether in mid-America, East Africa, or Southeast India, bear witness to his insights and teaching prowess on leadership. It's those years of stretching to make leadership live in the student's mind and heart that give birth to *The Genesis Principle of Leadership*. The age-old questions of "where" and "how" and "when" about leadership simply never found resolution in the plethora of pages.

*The Genesis Principle of Leadership*, as the name suggests, takes us back to the beginning. There's a direct relationship between the remarkable creative act of God and the leadership capabilities within each person. That relationship is intriguingly exposed and expanded in Dr. Allen's notions of the source of leadership. No longer do we need to discuss whether leaders are born or made—whether leadership is genetic or environmental. The source is The Source. Leaders simply reflect the characteristics God created within everyone.

If you're looking for the "tricks of the trade" or the newest spin on an old topic, read no farther. If you want a solid foundation on which to understand the beauty of leadership, a foundation on which to build a strong model for effective influence, then read on.

H. Charles Roost, Ph.D.<br>
Founder and Director, International Steward, Inc.<br>
Grand Rapids, Michigan

# Preface

Organizations don't collapse because there are not enough managers. Organizations collapse because there are not enough leaders.

Richard D. Allen

It's time to tell the truth about leadership!

The topic of leadership is all the rage these days. It seems as if our culture is obsessively gripped by some sort of primordial need for leadership. Even the most casual observer notices the astonishing explosion of books, articles, seminars, and websites devoted to this trendy topic. Over 2,400 books were published last year alone on leadership. The number is certain to increase this year. With such an explosion of interest, I've concluded that the best way to get a book published is to include the word "lead," "leader," or "leadership" in the title. To tell the truth, this is the reason I included the word "leadership" in the title of this book. Now admit it, isn't that the reason you purchased this book?

Frankly, I'm mesmerized by this alluring subject of leadership. I have been a professor of leadership and management since 1974. I've conducted hundreds of leadership development seminars and workshops involving thousands of organizational leaders across the country. I've conducted leadership courses and seminars in nearly fifty nations. I take every opportunity to visit my favorite bookstore, purchase a large cup of my favorite, albeit expensive, coffee drink (a double latte macchiato with heavy cream, extra cinnamon, and a dash of nutmeg—with whipped cream, when my wife is not looking), then scurry to the business section to scope out the latest releases on this fashionable topic. I am zealous to learn all I can about leadership.

Some book titles are intriguing: *The Seven Habits of Highly Effective People: Powerful Lessons in Personal Change;*[1] *The 8th Habit: From Effectiveness to Greatness;*[2] *The 9 Natural Laws of Leadership;*[3] *Lead to Succeed: Ten Traits of Great Leadership in Business and Life;*[4] *The 13 Fatal Errors Managers Make and How to Avoid Them;*[5] *The 17 Indisputable Laws of Teamwork: Embrace Them and Empower Your Team;*[6] *The 21 Indispensable Qualities of a Leader: Becoming the Person Others Will Want to Follow;*[7] and, *How to Think Like a CEO: The 22 Vital Traits You Need to Be the Person at the Top.*[8]

Other titles are downright disturbing, such as *The 48 Laws of Power.*[9] The Machiavellian approach to leadership espoused by this book is not about influencing people in a positive, winsome way. This book is what I call the "I'm here to pull you buzzards into the twenty-first century" approach to leadership. The *48 Laws of Power* is a book about cunning manipulation. It teaches people to do anything, anywhere, at anytime to get what they want regardless of how many people get hurt in the process. If there is any redeeming value to this book, it is to make one aware of the cunning, manipulative people out there masquerading as leaders.

Some titles are absolutely amusing: *Jackass Management Traits;*[10] *The 101 Dumbest Moments in Business;*[11] *The 108 Skills of*

*Natural Born Leaders;*[12] *Leading Every Day: 124 Actions for Effective Leadership;*[13] and, just when you think "124" traits tops them all, John Baldoni released his book, *180 Ways to Walk the Leadership Talk: The How to Handbook for Leaders at All Levels.*[14] It makes me wonder, what number is next? 360?

So, just how many leadership traits are there: 7? 8? 9? 10? 13? 17? 21? 22? 124? 180? And how fast can one become a leader? Some writers make the dubious claim that you can become a leader in as few as 60 seconds. Another author claims it can be done in as little as 10 seconds. And, not to be outdone, yet another author claims that you can become a leader "now."

In spite of this deluge of confusing advice about leadership, reports of massive corporate collapses continue to dominate the business headlines:

> AVS Sputters into Chapter 11
>
> Japan Registers Third-highest Number of Corporate Failures Since WWII
>
> Germany Posts 25% Rise in Corporate Failures
>
> Charges Filed in HP Spying Scandal
>
> Lucent Posts $7.9B Loss
>
> Tyco to Cut 7,100 Jobs, 24 Factories
>
> Delta to Cut 8,000 Jobs
>
> Kodak to cut 15,000

Global Crossing, Enron, Adelphia, WorldCom, Tyco, Kenneth Lay, Jeffrey Skilling, Andrew Fastow, and Patricia Dunn are all now infamous names representing colossal collapses in leadership. The consequences are felt globally: national economies weakened by the loss of thousands of employees and, through the loss of investors and creditors, have been brutally damaged, some fear irreparably. You and I suffer the consequences through rising costs at the gas pumps and supermarket checkout lanes. And yet the problem relentlessly persists: we continue to hear about corruption at the highest levels in corporations and governments around the world.

When a problem is this pervasive it must be systemic. Who or what is responsible? Is it the federal government? Is it the escalation of tensions in the Middle East? Are terrorists to blame? Or is it good old-fashioned greed that accounts for these large-scale leadership meltdowns? It is my conviction that organizations don't collapse because there are not enough managers; organizations collapse because there are not enough leaders. In the 1960s, the folksingers, Peter, Paul, and Mary, made popular a song that asked the question, "Where have all the flowers gone?" Perhaps today's headlines should cause us to ask, "Where have all the leaders gone?" As Peter, Paul, and Mary pondered, "Long time passing?"

Yet, in spite of the overwhelming need for strong leadership and notwithstanding our primordial obsession with leadership, there is little consensus about what makes for a good leader. Few topics are more hotly contested these days. Self-acclaimed leadership gurus are sharply divided over the issue of leadership. Indeed, there is a cacophony of contradictory voices clamoring for your attention and your credit cards.

By and large, the term leadership is defined in positional terms. That is, one is a "leader" because of title, rank, or position. Typically, anyone who is elected, selected, appointed, self-appointed, anointed, promoted, or deemed successful is regarded to be a leader. Frequently, a "leader" is portrayed as indispensable and charismatic, without whom the show cannot go on. A leader is one who graduated from the "right" school (such as Harvard, Michigan State University, or Covenant College), or works for the "right" organization (such as Wal-Mart, Ford Motor Company, or Microsoft). Patricia Dunn, for example, was touted as a "leader" because she was chairwoman of the Silicon Valley giant, Hewlett-Packard Company. But California's attorney general, Bill Lockyer, observing that Hewlett-Packard had "lost its way," filed charges against Dunn for violating state privacy laws in her attempt to root out the source of boardroom leaks. Frankly, most current definitions of leadership simply do not stand up in the light of these kinds of headlines.

*Webster's Ninth New Collegiate Dictionary* defined a leader as "one who has the ability to lead, show the way to, guide the course or direction of, or to be the first or foremost."[15] In other words, a leader is one who leads or is in the lead. This definition is not exactly helpful either and does not begin to exhaust pop culture's varying and elusive definitions. It is, nonetheless, indicative of a trend that distorts, confuses, and paralyzes contemporary notions about leadership. There is a vacuum of substantive, meaningful thought about leadership. The current debate is not producing solutions to our culture's leadership problem. Perhaps, Barbara Kellerman[16] was right, there is too much rubbish out there—too much ill-informed and misleading advice.

Unfortunately, this obsession with leadership is not unique to the secular culture. The faith-based community is equally enchanted with the current leadership craze. There is an explosive eruption of Christian publications, associations, seminars, and sermons focusing on leadership. Regrettably, a good deal of Christian thinking about leadership is woefully unexamined, oblivious to the deeply flawed philosophical notions of personhood driving much of the contemporary thinking about leadership. Consequently, some prominent Christian writers, leaders, and pastors recklessly ransack and adopt the latest leadership "flavor of the month," casually baptize these defective notions about leadership by sprinkling them with sloppily selected Bible verses, and then piously pronounce them as "the" Christian view of leadership.

Consequently, there is far too much misleading "Christian" advice out there. Though the Christian community resists secular thinking from the pulpit, it is unwittingly adopting secular notions in practice. The Christian community can ill afford to uncritically adopt trendy views about leadership driven by impersonal and reductionistic views about personhood if it is to effectively respond to its high calling in the twenty-first century. Frankly, there is a vacuum of Christian thinking about leadership. Christian colleges are notorious for "training the next generation of leaders" but turning out followers by the cage full—"rabbits"—as Solzhenitsyn might have called them. Thoughtful Christians must be directing the leadership debate, not straggling behind, "...tossed to and fro by the waves and carried about by every wind of doctrine..." (Ephesians 4:14, ESV). It's time to develop a biblical model regarding leadership. It *is* time to tell the truth about leadership!

Hopefully, *The Genesis Principle of Leadership* is much more than just another one of the 2,400 books about leadership published this year. While unapologetically entering the current fracas about this important topic, my hope is that *The Genesis Principle of Leadership* represents a sincere attempt to work out and begin, even establish a truly biblical approach to the age-old question, "Are leaders born or made?" Toward that end, I will build upon one of the central, but often avoided, canons of historic, orthodox, biblical Christianity, the doctrine of *imago Dei*. That is, God made man to be His image. (You and I are sons and daughters of the living God. Thus the generic use of masculine words like "man" or "person" used throughout this book is to be interpreted as "human being"—both male and female. I trust that the context in which these words are used will make each pronoun clear.)

You were made by God to be His image:

> Then God said, "Let us make man in our image, after our likeness. And let them have dominion over the fish of the sea and over the birds of the heavens and over the livestock and over all the earth and over every creeping thing that creeps on the earth." So God created man in his own image, in the image of God he created him; male and female he created them. And God blessed them. And God said to them, "Be fruitful and multiply and fill the earth and subdue it and have dominion over the fish of the sea and over the birds of the heavens and over every living thing that moves on the earth."
>
> Genesis 1:26–28 (ESV)

Each and every person possesses, in equal portion, the created attributes imparted to them by God in His incomparable act of creation. Leadership characteristics emerge from these God-given attributes. Consequently, and contrary to popular belief, leaders are not born; leaders are not made. Leadership is not the byproduct of the genetic code, nor is leadership the product of having grown up in the "right" environment or having attended the "right" college. Leadership has nothing to do with being the CEO of a Fortune 500 company. Rather, leaders are created. Leadership arises directly from the attributes of God. Because every person, male and female, is created to be God's image, every person, male and female, possesses equal capacity and full potential for effective leadership. In short, you and I possess, right now, the right stuff for leadership.

There's more. Because you and I are created in God's image, we share, equally, the responsibility to bear God's image. That is, we are to rediscover and cultivate the long-forgotten created attributes of God. We have been charged with the responsibility to carry each one of these created attributes, leadership traits, into every arena of our personal and professional lives. When we reflect God's created attributes, we are leading. Leadership, then, is best defined as "claiming and cultivating the created attributes of God." This is our created capacity for leadership; this is the *Genesis Principle of Leadership;* this is the truth about leadership.

The purpose of this book is three-fold. First, I want you to be able to identify, reclaim, and cultivate your created capacity to lead. Second, I want to stimulate further thinking about leadership by reflective and visionary people eager to make a difference. Third, it is my hope that much of the current confusion about leadership, particularly in the Christian community, can be corrected by means of a careful, biblical evaluation of the popular notions about leadership. Leadership that is biblically understood and practiced will have a fundamental impact on how we competently identify and cultivate capable leaders at home, school, work, church, and community. It is important to remember, though, that any work of this sort must be viewed as a starting point, a work in progress, and subject to examination and refinement in the light of a greater understanding of the biblical revelation and increased understanding and insight of the general revelation. I invite such scrutiny and dialogue.

There are three things that will help you benefit by reading *The Genesis Principle of Leadership.* First, read each chapter carefully. Take your time. Allow the ideas and principles discussed in each chapter to penetrate your mind and your imagination. Some ideas will excite and motivate you. Other ideas will challenge you. Perhaps some ideas will anger you. Write your thoughts, responses, and questions in the margins. Intentionally engage and interact with each paragraph of this book.

Second, reflect on what you encounter in the pages of this book. Use the "Personal Reflection" section at the end of each chapter to help guide your reflection(s) regarding what you have read. Record your responses, answers, and ideas. Again, don't be in a hurry. Rediscovering and cultivating your created capacity for leadership calls for a life-long commitment. There are no shortcuts. There is no "10-second formula" for success. But if you don't begin—today—you can never finish. You will not become the leader God created you to be. Declare today as your starting point for rediscovering, claiming, and cultivating your creative capacity for transformational leadership.

Third, respond to the principles of leadership identified in this book by completing the "Cultivating Your Created Leadership Capacity" section found at the end of chapters 3–14. What are you going to do with what you learn in each chapter of *The Genesis Principle of Leadership?* For what you "do" with what you learn is what true knowing is all about. In other words, how are you going to steward your created leadership capacity? Once again, take your time. But—take action! Implement each attribute. In other words, go out and lead!

God intends you to be the leader you were created to be—leading in your home, church, work, and community. He created you with the full capacity to be an effective leader. He has given you His *Genesis Charge.* Begin, today, to claim and cultivate your created leadership attributes. In so doing, you will "... take hold of that which is truly life" (I Timothy 6:19, ESV).

So get ready! It's time to know the truth about leadership!

God bless you as you begin this remarkable quest toward a full, free, fruitful, and fulfilling life as the leader you were created to be.

# The Quest for Leadership

> Until philosophers rule in the republic or kings and rulers seriously and successfully pursue wisdom—unless political power and the love of wisdom unite and those people who follow only one of them are categorically excluded—neither republics nor the entire human race will ever be free from corruption. Until that happens, the republic we have been creating will never come to life and see the light of day.[17]

## An Age-old Topic

Leadership is an age-old topic. God's first instruction to Adam and Eve upon the dawn of creation was to lead, to "...have dominion" (Genesis 1:28, ESV). Abraham led his family out of Ur of the Chaldeans (Genesis 12:1-6, ESV). Nearly fifteen centuries before the birth of Jesus Christ, Moses led millions of his fellow Israelites out of Egypt. Moses, revered by many to be one of the most famous leaders in history, delivered the Israelites from slavery and led them to freedom in the land of Canaan.

Confucius (551? - 479? BC), a formative philosopher and social theorist in the history of Chinese thought, established principles of leadership based upon the five character virtues of kindness, uprightness, decorum, wisdom, and faithfulness. The Greek philosopher, Plato (428?-347 BC), one of the most creative and influential intellects in the history of western thought, felt strongly about the importance of leadership. In his famous work, *The Republic,* Plato[18] described an ideal republic where philosopher-kings would provide wise and judicious leadership. To support this ideal, Plato established the Paidea, a school designed to develop such philosopher-kings for his utopian republic.

Jesus Christ, the central figure of Christianity, spoke often about leaders and leadership. Shortly before his crucifixion, Jesus cautioned his disciples about poor leadership warning,

> For false christs and false prophets will arise and perform great signs and wonders, so as to lead astray, if possible, even the elect.
>
> Matthew 24:4 (ESV)

Nevertheless, important questions about leadership continue to be asked today with a heightened sense of urgency. What is the underlying apparatus that drives leadership? Is it genetics? Is it the environment? Is it attending the "right" school? Is there some primordial soup that explains "leadership"? What do first-rate leaders possess that separates them from the rest of the pack? Can leadership be taught? Or is leadership caught? Are leadership skills transferable? What is at the core of effective leadership? Am I a leader? How can I become a more effective leader?

There is an enormous body of conflicting and disparaging views on each of these questions. Unfortunately, most fail to answer these crucial questions about leadership. Thus far, most leadership models have failed to provide an adequate description for effective leadership. One only needs to read today's headlines. Is there not a view of leadership that can really make a difference in the twenty-first century?

## An Age-Old Question

"Tell me, Richard. You're a college professor. Are leaders born or made?"

I was startled by this peculiar greeting. Actually, I was flabbergasted. It's true. I am a college professor. I teach management and leadership courses at Covenant College, high atop Lookout Mountain, near Chattanooga, Tennessee. I was calling on a senior executive of a large foundation to express appreciation for the foundation's long-standing and generous financial support of the college. As I entered the door into his luxurious, well-appointed, mahogany-paneled office, I was greeted with his bewildering question.

Not one to shy away from a first-rate challenge, I retorted, "Made! This is what Covenant College is all about! We're in the business of making leaders!" Frankly, I felt rather smug with my quick-witted comeback. What followed could be described as gracious, just as easily as spirited. This highly regarded community leader and I took opposing stances on this age-old question.

"Leaders are made!" I said.

"Leaders are born!" he exclaimed. "Your position is not biblical!"

We soon ran out of time, forgetting the original purpose of our scheduled appointment. Though befuddled by this executive's unanticipated challenge and relentless interrogation (he is an attorney by training), his provocative greeting prompted what has grown into my zealous pursuit for a balanced and reasoned response to this troublesome, question, "Are leaders born or made?"

## So Tell Me—Are Leaders Born or Made?

Brad VanPelt was unquestionably the greatest athlete ever to come out of the farm country of mid-Michigan. Brad earned eight varsity letters in football, baseball, basketball, and track and field at Owosso High School. In his senior year he was named all-state quarterback and given honorable mention on the Sunkist *All-American High School Basketball Team*. Brad had enormous strength. In high school track and field, he threw the shot put 46 feet, 7 inches. Brad's "Number 10" football jersey, now retired, hangs in the halls of Owosso High School.

All around town people say, "What a natural born athlete!"

Brad attended Michigan State University where he was a three-sport athlete, receiving collegiate letters three times in football and twice in baseball and basketball. He earned numerous honors from *The Associated Press, Walter Camp Foundation, United Press, The Sporting News, Time Magazine, American Football Coaches Association, Football Writers Association, Football News, Universal Sports, The Columbus Touchdown Club*, and others. Brad became the first defensive back—ever—to receive the *Maxwell Award* as the nation's top collegiate player. He was a second-team *All-Big Ten* pick in baseball as a pitcher and still ranks eighth on the Michigan State single-season strikeout list. When Brad played baseball at Owosso High School, one major league baseball team scout said, "No major league pitcher can throw the baseball as hard as Brad!"

"What a natural born athlete!"

Though drafted into professional baseball, Brad decided, instead, to play professional football. He was drafted in the first round by the New York Giants playing fourteen years in the National Football League (New York Giants for ten years, Los Angeles Raiders for three years, and the Cleveland Browns for one year). He played in five straight Pro Bowls and was named player of the decade for the 1970s by the Giants.

"What a natural born athlete!"

Brad continues to be honored for his athleticism. Brad was named to the *Lansing State Journal's* Michigan State University's Centennial Super Squad in 1996; inducted into the *MSU Athletics Hall of Fame* in 2000; inducted into the *Michigan Sports Hall of Fame* in April, 2002; and inducted into the *College Football Hall of Fame* in December, 2002.

"What a natural born athlete!"

Or was he?

You see, the only thing most people saw were Brad's amazing athletic accomplishments on game day. Brad grew up in my neighborhood. Few people observed the countless hours he spent practicing and training—shooting thousands of free throws—often after dark—into the old backboard suspended over the garage door; pitching the baseball—again and again and again—into his father's well-worn catcher's glove; or, throwing the football, with laser precision, through the old rubber tire dangling from the tall burr oak tree in his backyard.

So, was Brad Van Pelt a natural born athlete—or was he made?

This is the very question that divides us on the topic of leadership, "Are leaders born or are leaders made?" The nature camp contends that leaders are born. That is, some people are genetically encoded to be successful leaders. The genetic material, DNA, is not only the "puppet master" of the color of your eyes and skin, but also pulls the strings of your behavior and leadership abilities. Some inherit leadership capability by birth; others, it seems, do not.

The nurture camp, on the other hand, claims that the genetic material is not the fundamental building block of life. Rather, leaders are made. The environment shapes and molds your behaviors, likes, dislikes, and leadership capacity. Some catch leadership because of the advantages of living and growing up in a particular environment; others are not leaders because they had the misfortune of growing up in a less nurturing environment.

More recently, others suggest that there is a shared or interdependent relationship between DNA and the environment. The genetic material interacts with and alters the environment; the environment interacts with and alters the genetic material. This suggests that leadership is a by-product of the interdependence of what were once thought to be independent and competing factors. So the question remains, are leaders born, made, or "cooked"?

## Simply a Machine

This boiling cauldron of conflicting views about the source of leadership emerged out of the popular and fashionable view of personhood known as behaviorism. Behaviorism, with its philosophical roots in the revolutionary work of the famous seventeenth century philosopher Rene' Descartes (1592–1650), is the driving force for most current notions about human beings in the fields of sociology, psychology, education—and leadership. Popularized by the likes of Sigmund Freud (1856–1939), John B. Watson (1878–1958), and B. F. Skinner (1904–1990), behaviorism claims that the mind of man is nothing more than another organ that simply reacts to random stimuli from the external environment. The person is not a free-acting and independently responsible agent. Rather, a person's behavior is the accumulation of biological responses to various chemical and physical stimuli. Human behavior, therefore, is best studied and understood through chemistry, physics, and mathematics. The human brain is simply a machine, just another infinitely small part of

Descartes' "vast machinery of the universe." David Cohen summarized behaviorism this way:

> The central tenet of behaviorism is that thoughts, feelings, and intentions, mental processes all, do not determine what we do. Our behavior is the product of our conditioning. We are biological machines and do not consciously act; rather we react to stimuli. [19]

Sigmund Freud, physiologist, medical doctor, and father of psychoanalysis, remained convinced that the mind was nothing but a machine—understandable only through the sciences. The notion that man had a mind or soul was nothing more than a ridiculous metaphor—pure fiction for Freud. Though he was never able to scientifically prove his position, Freud did admit, late in life, that there was a "ghost in the machine." But notice he still viewed man as a machine.

This notion, that human beings are simply part of the vast machinery of the universe, remains one of the underlying philosophical views of our culture today—driving most notions about the nature of human nature. The acclaimed scientist, C. U. M. Smith was much more assertive than Freud:

> There are no ghosts in the brain's machinery, no unmoral movers. It is all a matter of physics and chemistry. An understanding of the burgeoning brain science of our times depends on a prior knowledge of the thermodynamics of ions, membranes, and aqueous solutions. It is from an understanding of events at this level that the dawning comprehension of the entire system stems. It is only from this background that the nature of the nerve impulse,

synaptic transmission, and sensory transduction can be understood. And it is a combination of these phenomenons, which makes the ongoing activity of our brains. [20]

The consequences of this widely held view of the person are catastrophic. The classical and traditional explanations of man have been methodically replaced with mathematical and scientific models that have reduced personhood to a mere machine describable only by chemistry, physics, and mathematics. Gone are the once trusted notions that explained the uniqueness of the person through personal intentions, desires, thoughts, feelings, and will. Individuality is lost. The traditional view of personhood is gone. Man is reduced to comparisons to the latest supercomputer—a Cybersapien.

Indeed, such naturalistic views of personhood pervade every arena of human life. Much of what takes place today in the fields of psychology, sociology, education, medicine, and leadership theory is driven by, and reflects the biases of, this pervasive view of the person. Little wonder that David Brooks would conclude,

> We once thought that children were shaped by God. But as the twenty-first century dawns, this notion is becoming more of a fallacy. We know that children are shaped by the interaction of their DNA and their environment. [21]

## Insidious Assault

Leadership trends over the past 100 years clearly reflect this insidious assault on the person. Leadership models including the Trait Theory of the early 1900s (the first formal leadership model), the style theories of the 1940s, the behaviorist theories of the 1960s, and the contingency models of the 1980s and 90s, and others, have each attempted to identify either the genetic or the behavioral traits of effective leaders. Batteries of extensive tests were developed by which prospective leaders were scientifically assessed and identified. Tens of thousands of people were shuffled to elaborate hotels and retreat centers to be trained (or conditioned) in how to succeed as leaders.

Some leadership models became downright trendy. But each faddish model collapsed just as suddenly as it appeared only to be replaced by the latest leadership "flavor of the month." No one was able to identify what, if anything, successful leaders held in common. Trait Theory models, for example, collapsed when the only conclusion reached by numerous elaborate studies revealed that effective leaders were either above or below average height. This left those looking for the most effective model of leadership overwhelmed and confused.

As the twenty-first century opens, a bizarre and eclectic assortment of approaches to leadership is emerging. Early models of leadership are being ransacked, rearranged, and reconfigured into an assortment of beguiling and provocative concoctions of leadership characteristics considered to be "vital" to successful leadership. Each one promises "instant success" simply by adopting and mimicking a new set of prescribed behaviors. But the questions remain, "What characteristics are essential to effective leadership?" "Where do these traits come from?" "Are leaders born or made?" "How do I know if I have the right stuff for leadership?"

## Christian Rubbish

Unfortunately, mechanistic views about leadership do not stop here. Reductionistic notions of personhood are creeping into and distorting the classical Christian beliefs about the person. The Christian community is obsessively riding this surging leadership tidal wave. There is an explosive propagation of leadership books, articles, seminars, sermons, associations, and leadership centers purporting to be "Christian."

However, a careful examination reveals an extremely dangerous problem with much of the leadership material purporting to be "Christian." In far too many instances, the latest leadership "flavor of the month," driven, as I have shown, by a low, reductionistic view of the person, is uncritically adopted then "baptized," as it were, with a sprinkling of carelessly selected and misapplied Bible verses. These "sanctified" leadership models are then recycled as the "authentic" Christian view of leadership. Unfortunately, these so-called "Christian" views of leadership are merely passed through the blender of behavioristic thinking with little recognition of the subtle and dangerous mechanistic philosophical framework underlying most of the current notions about psychology, sociology, education, and, especially leadership. As a result, there has been a regrettable pandemic of Christian publications, seminars, and sermons that advocate deplorably defective and unbiblical, perhaps anti-biblical, notions about leadership.

This is serious business. The very notion about the nature of the person is at stake. Few Christians are able to discern the differences between sanctified secularism and genuine biblical leadership. This is such a pervasive problem that a colleague once asked, "How do I help my students see the differences between applied humanism with a sanctified coating and genuine biblical leadership?"

There is too much Christian rubbish out there. It's time to explore and develop a biblical framework for leadership. It is time to redeem current thinking about the true nature of man by developing a biblically informed response to the prevailing, reductionistic views of personhood with its implications for leadership.

It's time to tell the truth about leadership.

# Personal Reflection

## *The Quest for Leadership*

- Who do you know—personally—that is an excellent leader?

- List some of the most notable leadership traits of this person.

- Which trait do you admire most in this individual? Describe an incident in which this trait was evident.

- Where did these traits come from? Nature? Nurture? What are your thoughts?

- Do you think you possess any of the leadership traits of this person? Which one(s)?

- Do you think you have the capacity for leadership? Why? Why not?

- List some of your particular leadership traits:

# CREATED TO LEAD

What makes you who you are?
(What is) the potent shaper of the human essence?[22]

## What is Man?

David was king of the most powerful nation in the world. He was the consummate warrior—no stranger to combat. As a young boy he challenged and killed the horrific giant, Goliath, sending the dreaded Philistine army into a frenzied retreat. Throughout his life David confronted and crushed numerous bands of marauders, militants, and mighty armies. He was known throughout the region for his great prowess in battle and vast military resources.

At the height of his military career, and, perhaps, just as he ascended the throne as king of Israel, David reflected on what God had done for him and his people. He praised God for strengthening and protecting him as he faced his enemies. In his praise, David ascribed to God several of his most cherished descriptions: *My Rock; My Fortress, My Stronghold, My Deliverer,* and *My Shield* (Psalm 144:1–2, ESV). Then, in the midst of his jubilant celebration of God's greatness, David paused to ponder the profound philosophical problem that has perplexed people throughout the ages, "O Lord, what is man that you regard him, or the son of man that you think of him?" (Psalm 144:3, ESV).

"What is man?" Sounds familiar doesn't it? In other words, what makes a person a person? What makes me, me? It's the same soul-searching question you and I have posed again and again and again. You are not the only person who has asked this vexing question. The pursuit for an answer to this nagging question has been the pursuit of every person in every culture and every generation since the dawn of creation. Indeed, this is not an abstract question reserved exclusively for theologians, philosophers, and literary giants. Countless novels, plays, and music releases have pondered this perplexing question. Kansas, the popular rock and roll band of the 1970s, offered a pessimistic response to this question when they sang:

> Dust in the wind.
> All we are is dust in the wind.
> Dust in the wind.
> Everything is dust in the wind.

## Insidious Attack

What is man? What makes a person a person? What makes me, me? Today, there is an intellectual and cultural battle raging over the answer. Led by the naturalistic philosophies and the human sciences, the traditional Judeo-Christian view of the person is under severe attack. In fact, personhood itself is under attack. The uniqueness of your personhood is being assaulted, discounted, distorted, and destroyed by technology, bureaucracy, mass media, the behavioral sciences, the judicial system, and even by recent advances in the field of biomedicine, such as artificial insemination, cloning, genetic engineering, abortion, and euthanasia. It seems that the machine of modern society is geared to absorb individuality and rob your human uniqueness. Naturalistic views that distill the human mind to nothing more than the boom and buzz of electrical impulses and chemical reactions devalue life in general and, specifically, humanity.

The image of personhood that is emerging, particularly from the behavioral sciences, is radically distorted and far removed from the traditional and classical views of personhood. The prevailing view of the person is devoid of any concept that man is dependent on, or responsible to, a Creator God. As Stephen Evans described it,

> It is fair to say that the rise of the human sciences in the twentieth century has been marked by the demise of the person. That is, there is a definite tendency to avoid explanation of human behavior which appeals to the conscious decision in favor of almost any non-personal factors. The idea that God is the Creator of all things is forgotten. [23]

## The Answer

A correct understanding of personhood is not merely a cold, obscure, and irrelevant religious dogma. It is a foundational and indispensable part of understanding who you are and your sense of self-worth and dignity. It opens the door to purposeful living, to a proper understanding of self, and ultimately determines your view of leadership.

The classic, Judeo-Christian view of personhood starts with

an understanding of God Himself. The biblical record begins with God, "In the beginning God…" (Genesis 1:1, ESV). God alone is the fountainhead of all that exists. God is completely independent of and sovereign over all things He created. God is not dependent upon any created thing. Throughout eternity it is God alone who creates, upholds, and governs every part of His creation from the largest to the smallest. All reality is created by, owned by, controlled by, and completely dependent upon God. As the Apostle Paul wrote to the Christians in Rome, "For from him and through him and to him are all things. To him be glory forever. Amen" (Romans 11:36, ESV).

This means that God is the author of mankind. Furthermore, God is the author of personhood—your personhood. Again the biblical record is crystal clear:

> Then God said, "Let us make man in our image, after our likeness. And let them have dominion over the fish of the sea and over the birds of the heavens and over the livestock and over all the earth and over every creeping thing that creeps on the earth." So God created man in his own image, in the image of God he created him; male and female he created them.
>
> Genesis 1:26–27 (ESV)

Yes, you are a creature, part of the rest of God's creation. Yet, at the same time, you are set apart from the rest of creation. You are unique, carefully shaped, male and female, in the very image and likeness of God. Consequently, you are distinct from the rest of creation. This likeness is not incidental. It is intentional. It was God's conscious and purposeful design to make you in such a way that you reflect His image. In fact, being made in the image of God is the primary organizing principle of human life.

It is the essential element of your existence. It shapes how you are to live. People should be able to look at you and see something of God because you are to represent something of God Himself. You reflect Him, like a mirror, to the rest of creation. Indeed, reflecting God's image has significant implications for every person in every arena of life, including leadership. As Hoekema observed,

> Any view of the human being that fails to see himself or herself as centrally related to, totally dependent on and primarily responsible to God falls short of this truth. [24]

"What is man?" Man is the bearer of the very image of God. This is the answer!

## The Image Marred

Regrettably, your personhood was thoroughly corrupted through Adam and Eve's fall into sin. The Bible reveals that Adam and Eve failed to obey God (Genesis 3). Adam and Eve's rebellion, their fall into sin, impacted all of mankind and, consequently, the entire world. Sin entered the entire human race through Adam and Eve. Just as Adam and Eve's responsibility to reflect God was designed to impact every part of life, so too, man's rebellion against that responsibility impacts every part of life.

However, all is not lost. God's image in you, though marred and distorted by sin, is still intact. The consequence of the fall was to pervert and distort, but not completely destroy or eliminate God's image. You are what noted Christian apologist Francis Schaeffer called, "glorious ruins." You are still human with all of God's created, albeit distorted, attributes. In fact, it is impossible to be human without reflecting God's image in some facet of your life. Despite the ruinous effects of sin, you still gloriously bear the image of God. As Hoekema explained,

> Man is the highest creature God has made, an image bearer of God, who is only a little lower than God, and under whose feet all of creation has been placed. All this is true despite man's fall into sin. Thus... fallen man still bears (possesses) the image of God. [25]

It is important, at this point, to make clear, perfectly clear, that we are not God. We are only a likeness or reflection of God's image. Yet, we are called, in spite of our fallenness, to bear His image. We are to reflect God's likeness and character in every arena of life, at home, at school, at work, and at the shopping center.

## Charged to Lead

Your calling to bear the image of God has a profound impact on the way you are to approach the task of leadership. As an image bearer, God commands you to be a leader. In the opening verses of the Bible, God issued His *Genesis Charge:*

> And God blessed them. And God said to them, "Be fruitful and multiply and fill the earth and subdue it and have dominion over the fish of the sea and over the birds of the heavens and over every living thing that moves on the earth."
>
> Genesis 1:28 (ESV)

"Have dominion!" God commands you to take charge. At the very creation of the world, you were given the mandate to exercise dominion, lead, over the entire creation. In other words, you, made to reflect the image of God, were put in charge of the creation. You were given the authority to care for it, to protect it, and to foster its growth. However, this authority is not your own. It is derived from the God who made everything, and who, therefore, has ownership rights over all things. You were placed by God Himself in the principal position of leadership over His entire creation.

This gives you great dignity and tremendous responsibility. As a bearer of God's image, your duty, your charge, is to reflect the righteousness and purity of God's rule in every arena, large and small, of your life. You are to lead the creation for God, but only in a way that is consistent with His character—His attributes.

Understanding this doctrine is vital for a true understanding of leadership. You were created in the image of God so that you might reflect His image, as a leader, over the entire creation. God gave you most of His attributes so that as you properly reflect the righteousness and purity of those attributes, the earth might know and be filled with His glory. You accomplish this high and holy calling by actively rediscovering, claiming, cultivating, and applying your created, God-given attributes.

God's mandate, His *Genesis Charge,* has not changed. You are still commanded to fill the earth with the glory of God and rule over it. Yes, sin has wreaked havoc on your ability to be faithful to this mandate. Sin has perverted the righteous and pure attributes of God entrusted to you. The consequences can be catastrophic, often global. Fortunately, the biblical record does not end with fallen man condemned to a futile, desperate struggle to bear God's image with little hope of succeeding. That which was perverted, the created attributes of God, has been redeemed. God, through the death, burial, and resurrection of His Son, Jesus Christ, has redeemed your distorted and feeble attempts to portray His image. The effects of the fall are being reversed. Your charge to bear God's image has been renewed—

reissued, as it were. Through Christ, you have been reinstated, recharged, to be God's image-bearing leader.

Bearing the image of God is your created task; bearing the image of God is your fallen task; and, bearing the image of God is your redeemed task. This image, though already perfectly redeemed, is not yet perfectly restored. It will not be perfect until the perfect kingdom comes. Although redeemed, your work to reflect the image of God is not perfect. Nevertheless, your task remains. You must seek to fill the creation with the glory of God by reflecting His righteous rule in your leadership over your corner of the creation.

Bearing the image of God remains the major organizing principle of human life. The original goodness of creation, distorted by the fall, is being recovered through the process of redemption. As an image bearer of God, you play a central role in that process. The goal of the redemption of God's people is that you will be fully conformed into the image of Christ, the perfect image of God, the One whose image (glory) you are reflecting. John Calvin (1509—1564),[26] the French reformer and theologian observed,

> The image of God, which had been effaced by sin, may be stamped anew upon us, and that the advancement of this restoration may be continually going forward in us during our whole life because God makes his glory shine forth in us little by little. For we now begin to bear the image of Christ, and we are daily being transformed into it more and more, but that image depends upon spiritual regeneration. But (at the time of the resurrection) it will be restored to fullness, in our body as well as our soul; what has now begun will be brought to completion, and we will obtain in reality what as yet we are only hoping for.

## What You Do With What You Know

The image of God, the *imago Dei,* is not just a matter of what man is, what man was created to be, it is also a declaration of what man is supposed to do, what man was created to accomplish. You are a special creature of God with dignity not given to any other creature. Therefore, your responsibility lies in actualizing, that is doing what the scriptures reveal God is and does. In order to fill the earth with the glory of God, you are to live, work, and function just like God. Just as God loves, you are to love; as God is creative, you are to be creative; as God is merciful, you are to be merciful; and, as God is free and responsible, you are to be free and responsible. Others should be able to look at what you do and see something of God. You do not merely possess the image of God; you *do* the image of God. You were created to actualize His image by claiming and cultivating this unique capacity that was given to you in the magnificent feat of creation.

In what ways are you like God? What attributes has God given to you so that you might fulfill this grand and noble task of reflecting His greatness and filling the earth with His glory throughout all the earth? What attributes of God should others actually see you doing? These attributes are too numerous to list and describe in detail. And there are attributes that God reserves only for Himself (such as *omnipotent, omnipresent,* and *omniscient*). Therefore, I have selected twelve attributes that are illustrative and crucial to your created charge to lead. Only in man, through the created attributes such as these, does God uniquely manifest His glory throughout the rest of creation. You now know the true source of your dignity and sense of self-worth. There is no higher calling than the privilege of responsibly rediscovering, claiming, and cultivating these God-given attributes as you go about your high and holy calling of transforming every corner of the creation for Christ:

- You are active and purposeful. You have the capacity to see beyond your current circumstances, to develop a vision for a preferred future, and then intentionally implement strategies that will change each circumstance in your life and the lives of those around you.

- You are rational. You have the intellectual capacity to discover, perceive, understand, and relate to the world in meaningful and intentional ways. You exercise sound judgment and common sense in implementing informed and practical solutions to life's challenges.

- You are creative. You are imaginative, insightful, ingenious, inventive, and intentional enabling you to evaluate, comprehend, and generate creative ideas, resources, solutions, and transforming actions.

- You exercise dominion. You have the ability to purposefully exercise your inherent power and authority over that which is around you—which God created—as a responsible steward.

- You are moral. You are capable of thoughts and actions that have principled qualities. Hence, your interactions and dealings with others can be properly designated as "right" or "wrong."

- You are relational. You are created for intentional and interpersonal relationships emphasizing high regard for the well-being and personhood of others.

- You are free and responsible. You possess the ability to independently make meaningful choices, the freedom to act or not act out your choices, and the personal responsibility for the consequences of your decisions and actions.

- You are loving. You possess the ability to love and to be loved. By divine nature, calling, and duty you are to love God and others at all times by doing what is best for them and by practicing forgiveness.

- You are merciful. You are called upon to be actively gracious and compassionate toward the well-being and peace of others through acts of favor and mercy—even to those who do not desire or deserve it.

- You are faithful. You are to entrust your life, well-being, and soul to the faithful and true Creator. Similarly, others should acknowledge you as trustworthy and reliable as you faithfully do your work and good deeds. In this same way, you unreservedly view others as worthy of your trust, steadfastly relying upon them for the completion of the work.

- You are interdependent. You are totally and dynamically reliant upon God and your fellow human beings for your well-being and continued existence. Nonetheless, you remain irreducibly distinctive, independent, and irreplaceable with even greater individual capacity and influence, finding the center of your existence and significance in God and others.

- You are generous. You have the created capacity and responsibility to be generous as God is generous, dispensing the sacrificial grace of God to those around you by being supremely and wastefully generous with your time, talent, and treasure.

## Authentic Leadership

The point is this: leaders are not made; leadership is not the consequence of having been born, by a twist of fate, into the "right" environment, or of having had the good fortune of having attended the "right" college, or of having read the latest best-selling (fatally-flawed) book on leadership. Leaders are not born; leadership is not the product of mere chance or the roll of genetic dice. Rather, leaders are created. Leadership is found in and emerges from the created attributes. Genuine leadership ability emerges when you actively rediscover, claim, and cultivate these long-forgotten attributes of God. Because God has given you most of His attributes, you possess the full capacity for leadership. You were created in God's image. You possess His created leadership attributes. For this reason and this reason alone, you possess the "right stuff" for leadership. These created attributes make up the essential stuff of genuine leadership. Therefore, you possess the divine capacity for authentic leadership.

You have the created capacity to effectively respond to God's *Genesis Charge.* God's *Genesis Charge* is His mandate to carry God-given attributes of leadership into every arena of life. Structurally, you have been created as a leader. Functionally, you have been commanded to lead. You were created, charged, and equipped to lead. This *Genesis Charge* is your clarion call to get busy leading. As Os Guinness said, you are to "…lead in accordance with what you are…that is, how you are created."[27] You were created to exercise leadership attributes that reflect the righteousness and purity of God's rule. God made you for this purpose. This is the means by which the earth is filled with the glory of the Lord. This is your created capacity; this is your *Genesis Charge;* this is your high and holy calling, God's fullness, your wholeness, and your dignity. Your fruitfulness and fulfillment and freedom are wrapped up in bearing the image of God. This is the first and most important step to fully understanding the truth about leadership.

## Claim and Cultivate Your Leadership Capacity

Your essential task then is to claim and cultivate your created capacity for leadership. The renewal of the image of God within you is both a gift from God and your most important responsibility. Your duty, in reliance on the Holy Spirit, is to restore the long-lost image of God to its proper structure and function so that you can lead as God designed and charged you to lead. The problem with most of the prevailing notions about leadership, including many of those purporting to be *Christian*, is that they are not in harmony with this classical/biblical understanding of human nature nor the mandated role of reflecting the image of God. Rather, popular notions about the nature of human nature are misleading about leadership. The common creation of all men and women is for one great purpose—to fill the earth with the glory of God. The task of leadership is to take mankind back to this original end.

Enabling others to participate in the building of the City of God is another crucial task of leadership. That is, you are to disciple others in your spheres of influence to rediscover their created attributes and cultivate their exceptional capacity for leadership. You are to be God's instrument in allowing others to taste the greatness of Him. You must become more conscious of men and women as made in the image of God, possessing God-given leadership attributes, and sharing the responsibility to bear the image of God in their spheres of influence. The evolutionary forces of genetics or the developmental forces of the environment do not drive people. People are not in the process of perceiving, behaving, becoming the fully functioning self; people are not in the life-long pursuit of self-actualization or finding their own voice. Rather, your leadership development must be specifically directed at enabling each person to rediscover (structurally) the long-forgotten attributes of God and to cultivate (functionally) each attribute as leaders in their families, churches, workplaces, and community organizations. Your leadership must enable each person to restore every created attribute found in the image of God to its redeemed structure and function, to the greater glory of God. As a parent, pastor, teacher, supervisor, business owner, neighbor, or civic leader, you are to help others reclaim and cultivate the long-lost attributes of God.

You are a leader!

This is the truth about leadership!

This is the *Genesis Principle of Leadership!*

# Personal Reflection

*Created to Lead*

- What thoughts and feelings do you have when you reflect on the question, "What is man?"

- In what ways has your individual personhood been challenged?

- You are made in the image of God. What is the significance of this reality for you?

- Everyone you encounter is also made in the image of God. What are the implications of this reality for you?

- Being made in the image of God is the primary organizing principle of human life. How does this reality change life for you?

- As a righteous leader you are to seek to fill the earth with the glory of God. How might you do this in your home, workplace, church, and neighborhood?

- How do you respond to the idea that "leaders are created"?

- Do you believe that you have the "right stuff" for leadership?

# Leaders are Active and Purposeful

As a leader you have the capacity to see beyond your current circumstances, to develop a vision for a preferred future, and then intentionally implement strategies that will change each circumstance in your life and the lives of those around you.

## "We must act, act!"

Marie was obsessed with but one all-consuming ambition, to become a scientist. It seemed such a ridiculous idea for a woman growing up in Poland in the nineteenth century! There were just too many cultural obstacles—combined with too many personal calamities. Marie grew up in extreme poverty. One of her sisters, then her mother, died prematurely, forcing Marie to work as a private tutor to help with the family finances. At great personal sacrifice, Marie chose to help one of her sisters, Bronia, study medicine in Paris. It appeared as though Marie would have to abandon her passion to study science.

In spite of all these societal obstacles and personal tragedies, Marie did not permit any of these catastrophic events destroy her dream. In 1891, with the help of her sister, Bronia, Marie enrolled in Sorbonne in Paris to study science. She earned a degree in physics and soon another in mathematics. There she met Pierre, already an acclaimed scientist. Pierre proposed marriage in a letter writing how wonderful it would be for the two of them "… to spend life side by side, in the sway of our dreams: your patriotic dream, our humanitarian dream, and our scientific dream." Marie and Pierre Curie married in 1895.

As part of her doctoral studies in physics, Marie discovered several substances that emitted "x-rays." She coined the term "radioactive" to describe this phenomenon. Working in very crude and makeshift conditions, Marie and Pierre discovered that radioactive x-rays could be used to reduce the size of tumors. "Curietherapy" was started. Marie and Pierre received the Nobel Prize for Physics for their remarkable discoveries and applications of radioactivity.

Soon, sudden calamity struck yet another heartrending blow. In 1906, Marie's dearly loved husband, Pierre, was hit and killed by a car. Marie lost her adoring and devoted sweetheart. But she did not lose the humanitarian and scientific dream that brought them together. Marie continued her research and raised her two children—alone.

She also had to continue to fight the unrelenting prejudices of her day, including the hatred of foreigners (an everyday reality for a Pole living in France) and the bigotry against women in science. In 1911, she was not permitted to enroll in The Academy of Science because she was a woman. Even in the face of these maddening circumstances, Marie became the first woman to be appointed professor at Sorbonne, one of France's oldest and most esteemed universities. She received yet another Nobel

Prize, this time in Chemistry, for calculating the atomic weight of the radioactive element, Radium.

Tragedy struck yet again. War broke out. World War I, "the war to end all wars," only prompted Marie to exclaim to her daughter, Irene, "We must act, act!" With the help of her daughter, Marie found yet another use for x-rays, locating bullets and shrapnel in wounded soldiers. Her "X-ray Vans" saved thousands of lives during this tragic war. Not even a world war could destroy her passion for science or thwart her humanitarian aspirations.

After the war, Marie feverishly continued her research, discovering numerous other uses for radioactivity including the treatment of cancer, radiocarbon dating, molecular biology, and genetic engineering. In 1934, at the age of sixty-seven, Marie died of leukemia, a disease caused by handling too many dangerous, radioactive materials. Her passion for science cost her her life. In the face of numerous hardships and tragedies, Marie Curie paved the way for much of what happens today in the fields of nuclear physics and nuclear medicine. She was truly a woman of great determination, compassion, and courage.

Little wonder then that on April 21, 1995, Francois Mitterand, president of France, moved the remains of Marie Curie and her husband, Pierre, to the crypt beneath the dome of the Pantheon, France's magnificent memorial to illustrious Frenchmen. In this crypt lay the remains of France's most honored and revered countrymen: the philosopher Voltaire, writers Victor Hugo and Jean-Jacques Rousseau, the resistance fighter Jean Moulin, the politician Jean Jaures, and now, Marie and Pierre Curie. Thousands of people visit the Pantheon each day honoring the contributions that this Polish-born woman made to the prestige of scientific research in France.

## A Pioneer—Not a Victim

Marie faced countless challenges throughout her life: extreme poverty, the bigotry of her day, the heartbreaking loss of her husband, the devastation of a world war, and a life-ending disease. What power, gift, or trait enabled Marie to overcome so many unrelenting, social, political, economic, and personal hardships? Was it because she grew up in the right environment? Was it because she was born of good stock? No! In each and every life experience, no matter how trying, Marie was able to see beyond her circumstances. She developed a vision for a preferred future. Then Marie intentionally implemented strategies that changed each circumstance in her life and the lives of those around her. Her rallying call was, "We must act, act!"

Marie Curie refused to be a victim of her circumstances. Because she was active and purposeful, she chose to be a pioneer. This same attribute is given by God to every person in His incomparable act of creation. It is not a trait that only a few people, like Marie Curie, acquire through genetics. Nor is it a trait that just a fortunate few pick up from their environment. As unique, image-bearing creations of God, everyone is active and purposeful.

To be active and purposeful is an essential quality of leadership. Leaders are keenly aware of the circumstances around them, good, bad, ugly, and difficult. But as active and purposeful agents, leaders do not passively surrender and cave in to these conditions. Rather, leaders develop a vision for how things can, will, and should be different. In a very real sense, leaders can see into the distant future. They have the ability to analyze what is (or is not) and conceptualize, vividly see, what can be. Leaders intentionally design and implement the strategies necessary to achieve this hope, this longing, and this vision. Leaders see and shape a preferred future for themselves, their families, communities, and institutions.

## You Are Active and Purposeful

As a unique, image-bearing creature of God, you, too, are active and purposeful. Right now, you possess the full capacity to be active and purposeful in every situation in your life! Yes, your environment acts upon you, tragically at times. But you are not a helpless victim of life's circumstances. God made you to be His image. You possess the God-given ability to purposefully act upon your environment and each circumstance in your life. In fact, you have been charged to do so. You are to fill the earth, to subdue it, and to have dominion over it. You are to lead by being active and purposeful in every circumstance of your life. The trouble is that you may have forgotten that you possess this ability. This trait has atrophied from lack of use. Even so, being active and purposeful is a trait you are to rediscover and cultivate as an image bearer of God.

## Struck Down but Not Destroyed

Tammy Duckworth was a helicopter pilot in Iraq. During a routine mission, a rocket-propelled grenade exploded in the cockpit of her Blackhawk helicopter blowing both of her legs and part of one arm off. Miraculously, she was able to land her ship before passing out. At first, everyone thought she was dead—they thought they were simply recovering her body. Against all odds, Tammy survived. In 2006, the highly decorated Iraqi war veteran ran for U. S. Congress in the State of Illinois walking on two high-tech artificial legs. At one point in the campaign, she remarked, "The most difficult day on the campaign trail is nothing compared to learning to walk again." Though she lost the congressional race, Illinois Governor, Rod Blagojevich, appointed Tammy as the new Director of the Illinois Department of Veteran Affairs.

Like Tammy Duckworth—like Marie Curie—like everyone else, you will face a variety of difficult circumstances in your life. Some may be tragic. You may experience broken relationships—perhaps divorce, severe financial challenges, job loss, death of a dear friend or family member, a life-ending disease, serious injuries in an automobile accident, or lose everything in a tropical storm. Make no mistake about it—these are tragic circumstances. But because you were created to be active and purposeful, like God is active and purposeful, you will not have to cave in, a helpless victim of even the worst circumstance. How many times have you been inspired by stories of the likes of Tammy Duckworth, Marie Curie, and others who suffered tragic loss—but rose above their crushing circumstances to unbelievable accomplishments? I am reminded of the Apostle Paul's admonition to the Christians in the Church of Corinth:

> We are afflicted in every way, but not crushed; perplexed, but not driven to despair; persecuted, but not forsaken; struck down, but not destroyed.
>
> II Corinthians 4:8–9 (ESV)

## Cultivating Active and Purposeful Leadership

How do you go about rediscovering, claiming, and cultivating this essential leadership trait? First, recognize that you possess this trait. This trait was given to you by God when He created you. This is not a trait that you can purchase at the "Leadership Trait Shoppe." Nor is this a trait you will magically absorb by reading the latest best-selling book on leadership. Nor will you be able to acquire this trait by attending another expensive leadership seminar. This is not a trait that was fastened to your college diploma. The truth of the matter is—you *are* active and purposeful. You were created with this leadership attribute. Reckon this reality as real. Claim this trait, active and purposeful, for yourself.

Then cultivate this attribute. Put this essential leadership trait into action. In this way you will actually be active and purposeful. Take this leadership trait into every arena of your life: home, school, work, church, and community. Yes, there are challenging and difficult circumstances in each of these environments. Undoubtedly, there will be more challenges in your future. But you do not have to roll over and cave in to these life events. Remember—you are active and purposeful. Right now, you possess the ability to change your circumstances and to strategically develop a vision for a preferred future.

In fact, as a created leader, you are obligated to transform—actively and purposefully—every arena of your world. It is your "charge" to challenge and change every corner of your life for the honor and glory of Christ. You may not be able to change the whole world, but you can make an impact on your corner of the fallen world. As Clarissa Pinkola-Estes put it:

> Ours is not the task of fixing the world all at once but of stretching out to mend the part of the world that is within our reach. Any small, calm thing that one soul can do to help another soul, to assist some portion of this poor suffering world, will help immensely. [28]

You are active and purposeful. However, cultivating this leadership attribute will take time. Frankly, it will be a life-long pursuit. Reading, reflecting, attending seminars, enrolling in special courses and experimentation will be helpful. But there is one essential characteristic common to all who have successfully breathed new life into this leadership trait. Those who have been successful at being active and purposeful, start by being active and purposeful in their personal and professional lives. Such individuals have created a clear vision for their personal and professional future. They have developed a written plan for how they will change the circumstances in their environments.

There are a variety of other ways in which you can you rediscover and cultivate this core leadership trait. As a starting point, I recommend two activities that will help you become more active and purposeful. First, complete the "Personal Reflection" section at the end of this chapter. Take your time. Work slowly—intentionally. Reflect on your responses before recording them. Second, complete the "Cultivating Your Created Leadership Capacity" exercise at the end of this chapter. This activity will help you think through how to become more active and purposeful in each of your key life roles. These two activities will enable you to become a transformational leader. It will help you to cultivate your creative capacity to be active and purposeful in every arena of your life.

You are active and purposeful. You are a leader. This is the truth about leadership! This is the *Genesis Principle of Leadership*.

"You must act, act now!"

## Personal Reflection

*Leaders are Active and Purposeful*

- Leadership is reclaiming and cultivating your God-given, created attributes. What specific action steps will you take to develop this leadership trait: *Active and Purposeful?*

- What does it mean that God is active and purposeful in your life?

- List three ways in which God has been active and purposeful to you:

- List some specific actions you can take to be active and purposeful to others:

- Which action will you implement this week?

- To whom?

- What result(s) do you expect from taking this action?

- Take a few moments—now—to pray about this action.

- In what way(s) could you help someone in your family, workplace, or community to claim and cultivate this leadership attribute in his life?

- Continue to cultivate this created leadership trait by completing the "Cultivating Your Created Leadership Capacity" exercise on the next page.

## Cultivating Your Created Leadership Capacity

Leadership is the lifelong pursuit of claiming and cultivating your God-created attributes.

1. Select a Life Role (e.g. Leader, Spouse, Parent, Worker, Neighbor, etc.).
2. List the key Duties and Responsibilities of that Life Role.
3. Then design and list specific Action Steps that will enable you to steward this leadership attribute.

## Cultivating Active and Purposeful Leadership

As a leader you have the capacity to see beyond your current circumstances, to develop a vision for a preferred future, and then intentionally implement strategies that will change each circumstance in your life and the lives of those around you.

## Life Role:

_____

| Duties/Responsibilities: | Leadership is Action: |
|---|---|
| 1. | |
| 2. | |
| 3. | |
| 4. | |
| 5. | |
| 6. | |
| 7. | |

*What you do with what you know is what Christian knowing is all about.* (Os Guinness)

# Leaders are Rational

As a leader you have the intellectual capacity to discover, perceive, understand, and relate to the world in meaningful and intentional ways. You exercise sound judgment and common sense in implementing informed and practical solutions to life's challenges.

## Power to the Powerless

Oh what a fairy tale! From brewery worker—to stagehand—to dramatist—to prominent playwright—to essayist—to political dissident—to welder in a communist prison—then—president of Czechoslovakia! By his own admission Vaclav Havel was catapulted overnight into a world of fairy tales. Yet Havel insisted, in spite of the adamant claims of his adversaries, that he was just a normal person. His political foes said he was "not a normal man." Perhaps they were correct. For indeed, history itself may show that Vaclav Havel was the revitalizing intellectual figure and moral force that brought about the collapse of communism in Czechoslovakia and throughout Eastern Europe.

Vaclav was born in Prague in 1936 to wealthy parents.

Because of his parents' "bourgeois background," the controlling communist party declared the Havel family an "enemy of the state." Their property was confiscated. Vaclav was barred from attending university. All this, however, did not keep him from pursuing his intellectual and literary pursuits. He took full advantage of the massive family library, developing a keen interest in literature and poetry. As a young teen, Vaclav formed a literary circle called "Thirty-sixers," named after the year of the members' birth. He even dabbled in writing, publishing his first articles in literary and theatrical magazines.

Before long, Vaclav's writings took on a politically defiant slant. Over the next fourteen years he published numerous essays in which he intellectually criticized and challenged the oppressive communist establishment and its dehumanizing tactics to control the minds and souls of the people. He co-founded two activist human rights organizations, "Chapter 77" and "The Committee for the Defence of the Unjustly Prosecuted." The communists labeled his writings as "subversive;" his passport was confiscated, and his writings were banned.

Not to be deterred, Havel found another venue to voice his opposition to the communist bureaucracy, as a playwright. Eventually, however, his scathing reviews of the communist party and revolutionary activities earned him imprisonment. Vaclav was repeatedly harassed, arrested, and imprisoned for his "disloyal views" and "subversion of the republic." At one point, Vaclav was given the opportunity to leave the country instead of being imprisoned. He chose imprisonment, saying, "The solution of this human situation does not lie in leaving it."

Things began to escalate. Havel brought world attention to the struggles of his beloved homeland by writing an open letter to Alexander Dubcek, the Czechoslovakian president. In this brazen letter Vaclav wrote:

> So far, you and your government have chosen the easy way out for yourselves, and the most dangerous road for society: the path of inner decay for the sake of outward appearances; of deadening life for the sake of increasing uniformity; of deepening the spiritual and moral crisis of our society, and ceaselessly degrading human dignity, for the puny sake of protecting your own power.[29]

In 1989, Vaclav was imprisoned yet again for his open attacks upon the communist regime, this time for nine months. In spite of all these attempts to silence him, Havel emerged as the leading spokesperson of the human rights movement in Czechoslovakia. Internationally, he became recognized as the catalytic force in the Czechoslovak intellectual opposition.

In November of 1989, university students picked up the cause by organizing and leading massive anti-government demonstrations in Prague and in the smaller university city of Olomouc. On November 20, Havel encouraged the gathering crowd of nearly 500,000 people in Wenceslas Square in Prague to protest their resistance against the oppressive communist regime in spite of its threats to punish, even kill, the demonstrators. "Truth and love will always beat the lie and hatred." Vaclav's words kindled the flames of freedom for these young activists. Defiantly, the demonstrators rattled their key chains. It was both a beautiful and brave demonstration of their unity and resolve. One participant in this astonishing event told me that the communist soldiers, who had surrounded Wenceslas Square, fled in utter terror at the mere sound of the rattling keys. Within days this bloodless "velvet revolution" saw the collapse of the communist party in Czechoslovakia. Havel was immediately chosen as the interim president. Hundreds of thousands of people triumphantly celebrated Havel's inauguration with thunderous applause and deafening cheers, "Havel na hrad! Havel na hrad!" Havel to the Castle!

In 1990, Havel was re-elected and served as president of Czechoslovakia and then the Czech Republic for thirteen years. Vaclav retired from this office in 2003. He will be remembered throughout history as the one who brought power to the powerless.

## Living Rationally—Living Relevantly

Vaclav was correct. His life *was* a fairy tale. Regardless of how others viewed him (*elitist, intellectual, enemy of the state, not normal, subversive, bourgeois,* or *disloyal*), Vaclav always viewed himself as nothing more, or less, than an ordinary person, simply living normally, and attempting to do his work well. But how was this possible? The circumstances of his life were undeserved, wearisome, often discouraging. What quality, what character trait, enabled Havel to cope with his maddening circumstances and change the course of his life and world history?

Havel possessed the God-given ability to rationally and logically relate to the world about him. Though the circumstances in his life were often aberrant and perplexing, Vaclav was able to sort through and interpret those conditions, though bizarre at times, and generate new ideas and insights regarding these events. Then, based upon insightful and logical analysis, he formulated and implemented strategies that changed the circumstances of his life and the lives of those around him.

You are rational. This trait is not given to a select few, like Vaclav Havel. It is not given only to those with a good bloodline or those who had the good fortune of growing up in a good neighborhood. This is an attribute of God—given by Him to every single person. And you, like Havel, are endowed with the capacity to discover, perceive, understand, and intellectually relate to your world—though confusing, even maddening at times—in meaningful and purposeful ways. You possess the ability to exercise sound judgment and common sense, implementing informed and practical solutions to each one of life's challenges.

Living rationally is to live relevantly—to live purposefully. Living rationally is "the intellectually disciplined process of actively and skillfully conceptualizing, applying, analyzing, synthesizing, and/or evaluating information gathered from or generated by observation, experience, reflection, reason, or communication as a guide to belief and action."[30]

It is important to point out here that being rational transcends the mere accumulation of facts or the mastery of information. It is more than managing data and facts. Being rational is not the rote or mechanical use of data and skills with little or no concern for the consequences. This attribute is grounded in fair-mindedness and integrity. As Havel noted, "Its deepest roots are moral because it is responsibility expressed through action to and for the world."[31] In other words, being rational is being transformational, changing things for a purpose. As Os Guinness said, "What you do with what you know is what true knowing is all about."[32]

## So What Do You Do Now?

Contrary to today's reductionistic notions about human nature, rationality is universal. Every person is created rational. You were created rational. This means that you have the full capacity to be rational in each circumstance of your life. It is fundamental to all men and women. Therefore, it is an attribute that you must rediscover and cultivate. Certainly this attribute, like all the created attributes, has been terrifically distorted by the Fall. However, your fallen frailty does not excuse you from being a responsible bearer of this attribute of God.

Rational is an attribute that can be cultivated, grown, developed, refined, and matured. The cultivation of this attribute is, and must be seen as, a life-long process and undertaking. As William Graham Sumner observed over 100 years ago,

> This critical faculty is a product of education and training. It is a prime condition of human welfare that men and women should be trained in it. It is our only guarantee against delusion, deception, superstition, and misapprehension of us and our earthly circumstances. Education is good just so far as it produces this well-developed critical faculty. A teacher of any subject who insists on accuracy and a rational control of all processes and methods, and who holds everything open to unlimited verification and revision is cultivating this method as a habit in the pupils. Men educated in it cannot be stampeded... they are slow to believe. They can hold things as possible or probable in all degrees, without certainty and without pain. They can wait for evidence and weigh evidence... They can resist appeals to their deepest prejudices. Education in this critical faculty is the only education of which it can be truly said that it makes good citizens.[33]

Or as Vaclav Havel put it, being rational is "living the truth."

## Cultivating Rational Leadership

Cultivating this leadership attribute is intentional and conscious. It is hard work. It is a lifelong commitment to learning (both formally and informally through experience), to the application of that knowledge, and to re-learning what is forgotten. Allow me to suggest a few activities that will help you cultivate this important created leadership attribute.

First, as a starting point, complete the "Personal Reflection" exercise at the end of this chapter. Again, don't rush this activity. Take time to reflect on each question before recording your responses.

Second, complete the "Cultivating Your Created Leadership Capacity" exercise, also found at the end of this chapter. This exercise will enable you to think through the application of being rational in each of your life roles. Leaders are intentional observers of the human condition. Consequently, their work is directed to a purpose. Leaders are constantly trying to accomplish something, to change something, to improve the human condition. They are not maintainers, coasters, drifters, hangers-on. Leaders are determined to change the human condition for the better. Leaders have an aim in view; their thinking and their work is relevant to that purpose.

Third, seek out and pursue learning opportunities that will also help you cultivate this important leadership attribute—rational. Perhaps this means completing your college degree. Perhaps you need to enroll in that graduate program you have dreamed about for a long time. Frankly, there are just too many innovative programs out there that fit nicely into your learning style and busy lifestyle *not* to finish that degree. Perhaps you need to register for some professional or personal development seminars and workshops such as "Creative Problem Solving" or "Decision Making." Each of these "formal" learning options will help you cultivate this attribute—rational. Perhaps you would prefer a more informal approach. If so, consider reading books and journals, engage in intellectual conversations with colleagues, watch videos, listen to audio tapes, or other similar means. Whether you prefer a more formal or more informal approach, the end result must be that it aids the growth and maturity of this critical leadership trait.

Fourth, remember, "Leaders are readers." I realize that you've heard this before. But it's true! Leaders purchase and read books, all kinds of books, professional books, biographies, technical manuals, history books, and others—even if their employer will not reimburse them. Leaders realize how important reading is to the cultivation of their created leadership traits. Similarly, leaders subscribe to and read professional journals and magazines. Again, when necessary, leaders pay for these subscriptions out of their own pockets because they know how important it is to stay abreast of the unprecedented changes taking place in their field of expertise. Leaders take full responsibility for their own professional and personal development. Indeed, it is not unusual for leaders to read one or more books and two or more professional journals each month. Imagine—I know one leader who reads over forty books each year!

Each of these activities, and I'm sure you can think of some others, will help you cultivate your created capacity and to become a transformational leader in every arena of your life—the way God created you to be. Living rationally is to live relevantly.

You are rational. You are a leader. This is the truth about leadership! This is the *Genesis Principle of Leadership*.

# Personal Reflection

## *Leaders are Rational*

- Leadership is reclaiming and cultivating your God-given, created attributes. What specific action steps will you take to develop this leadership trait: Rational?

- What does it mean that God is rational?

- List three ways in which God has been rational to you:

- List some specific actions you can take to be rational to others:

- Which action will you implement this week?

- To whom?

- What result(s) do you expect from taking this action?

- Take a few moments—now—to pray about this action.

- In what way(s) could you help someone in your family, workplace, or community to claim and cultivate this leadership attribute in his life?

- Cultivate this created leadership trait by completing the "Cultivating Your Created Leadership Capacity" exercise on the next page.

# Cultivating Your Created Leadership Capacity

Leadership is the lifelong pursuit of claiming and cultivating your God-created attributes.

1. Select a Life Role (e.g. Leader, Spouse, Parent, Worker, Neighbor, etc.).
2. List the key Duties and Responsibilities of that Life Role.
3. Then design and list specific Action Steps that will enable you to steward this leadership attribute.

# Cultivating Rational Leadership

As a leader you have the intellectual capacity to discover, perceive, understand, and relate to the world in meaningful and intentional ways. You exercise sound judgment and common sense in implementing informed and practical solutions to life's challenges.

## Life Role:

_____

| Duties/Responsibilities: | Leadership is Action: |
|---|---|
| 1. | |
| 2. | |
| 3. | |
| 4. | |
| 5. | |
| 6. | |
| 7. | |

*What you do with what you know is what Christian knowing is all about.* (Os Guinness)

# Leaders Are Creative

As a leader you are imaginative, insightful, ingenious, inventive, and intentional enabling you to evaluate, comprehend, and generate creative ideas, resources, solutions, and transforming actions.

## Eureka! I Have Found It!

Archimedes of Syracuse, one of the greatest mathematicians of all times, lived and flourished in ancient Sicily in 287–212 BC. He developed and performed several geometric proofs and discovered ways of calculating the areas of complex geometric shapes, including the volumes of spheres and cylinders. Archimedes was also an excellent engineer. He invented the "Archimedean Screw" and discovered the law of the lever proclaiming, "Give me a place to stand and I will move the earth." Oddly, he discovered the law of buoyancy while taking a bath. Legend has it that he jumped out of the tub and ran through the streets of Syracuse shouting, "Eureka! Eureka!" meaning, "I have found it!"

Most likely, you've experienced bursts of creativity like this too. Perhaps, just like Archimedes, you were in your bathroom one morning, standing in front of the bathroom mirror preparing for work. Suddenly, like a flash of lightning out of nowhere, an outrageously creative idea erupted into your mind. Remember? Unfortunately, you probably did not act upon this ingenious idea. Then, regrettably, just a short time later, you learned that someone else became intensely wealthy, "over night," because he acted upon that very same revolutionary idea. How many times have you kicked yourself? You're not alone. We've all had a similar experience.

## What If?

I hear stories like this all the time. One morning King was standing in front of his bathroom mirror preparing to shave. But his old straight-edged razor was dull—again. In fact, his old razor was so dull and full of nicks that it could no longer be sharpened. It was useless and had to be thrown away. Suddenly, there was a flash of inspiration. "What if? What if there was a razor that did not need stropping every morning before using it? What if this razor could simply be thrown away when it became dull? What if this razor was safe to use—unlike the dangerous widow-making, throat-cutting straight razor?"

Well, the rest is history. Just five years later King Gillette started the Gillette Safety Razor Company. He became a multimillionaire and one of the most recognized celebrities around the world because his picture appeared on every box of disposable razor blades and safety razors sold. Today, the Gillette Corporation is one of the largest companies in the world, selling a variety of innovative products under such well-known names as Gillette, Braun, Oral-B, and Duracell.

## Who Knows, It Might Catch On!

In 1904, Antoine Ludwig Feutchwanger, *concessionaire extraordinaire*, was selling his homemade sausages at the Louisiana Purchase Exposition. Antoine called them "frankfurters" after his hometown, Frankfurt, Germany. He distributed white cotton gloves with each purchase so that his customers could enjoy his hot sausages without burning their fingers. Good idea! But this proved to be too expensive because his patrons did not return the gloves. So he gave each customer a porcelain plate instead. But the customers walked off with their "souvenir plates" too. Antoine's brother-in-law, a baker, had a flash of inspiration. "What if," he suggested, "I bake a long bun and slit it down the middle to hold the sausages? Then you can sell your franks and I can sell you the buns. Who knows, it might catch on!"

"Catch on?" What an understatement! Later one customer returned to order another frankfurter and yelled, "Give me another one of those hot dogs!" "Who knows, it might catch on." We smile whenever we think back on it, don't we? Hot dogs have become as much a part of American culture as baseball and apple pie.

## Created to be Creative

How is it that people are capable of generating creative solutions to problems and develop so many innovative products and services? How is it that people like Archimedes, King Gillette, Antoine Ludwig Feutchwanger, Bill Gates, and others are so innovative? Some tell us that these inventors were born creative. That is, creativity is found in the genetic code. Others tell us that their creativity was the product of having grown up in the "right" environment. So where does creativity come from?

The fact of the matter is that you were created to be creative.

The very God that used His remarkable, unsurpassed imagination and ingenious creative ability to form the day and the night, the galaxies and solar systems, the dry ground and the waters, and the plants and animals, also created you—the glorious and crowning achievement of His act of creation.

In His divine providence, God gave you this same creative ability. Procreation, the physical ability to have sexual intercourse to conceive children and produce more men and women, is an important dimension of this divine attribute. In fact, God commanded Adam and Eve to do so: "And God blessed them. And God said to them, 'Be fruitful and multiply and fill the earth...'" (Genesis 1:28, ESV).

But there is yet another critical aspect to fully appreciating this attribute. Like God, you are imaginative, insightful, ingenious, inventive, and intentional. God endowed you with the capacity to evaluate, comprehend, and generate creative and resourceful ideas, solutions, and actions. The result is that by mirroring God's creativity with your creativity, you are empowered to bring about relevant and beneficial change in the events, people, materials, and circumstances in purposeful and transforming ways. You were created to be a full participant in bringing God's kingdom to earth by filling the earth with His glory—through His created attributes.

## Inconceivable! But True!

God models this creative ability in numerous ways. But what possibly could compare to God's creative solution to man's fall from grace through the disobedience of Adam and Eve? Who could have imagined that He would spare no expense to make things right? Who would have thought that He would offer His one and only Son? And who could have dreamed that Jesus could be born of a virgin? Could God become incarnate? Could

God come in the flesh? Would God do this to serve us? Could Christ really be born to die, to be brutally crucified on a cross for the sins of the world, and then be raised from the dead so that those who would believe on Him would have the rights to be called "children of God?"

In the face of such mind-blowing creativity, you may feel like Vizzini in *The Princess Bride,* and want to scream, "Inconceivable!" Or perhaps like Indigo the Giant, you want to say, "You keep using that word, I do not think it means what you think it means." God's creative act of redemption is far beyond human comprehension. But it is, nonetheless, true. It is God's consummate creativity on full, magnificent display.

Likewise, it may seem "inconceivable" that God gave you this same creative capacity. But this too is true! You are made in His image. You possess most of God's attributes. You are creative because God created you to be creative. Therefore, you have the responsibility to faithfully rediscover and cultivate this leadership attribute, exercising it in every arena of your life: home, church, community, work, school, and play. You have the created capacity to act upon and change the events, people, materials, and circumstances about you in creative and transformational ways.

## The Truth of the Matter

Creativity is an essential leadership trait. Whether you like it or not, you happen to be living in a time when change is happening more rapidly than at any other time in human history. Unfortunately, this unprecedented pace of change is not going to get "better"—it's only to get "worse." At times you are being overwhelmed with tidal waves of new and increasingly specialized information; technology is outdated almost before it becomes available; you face a national and global economy that is fragile and unpredictable; and, businesses battle temperamental consumers whose demands and confidence seem to change by the hour. The success, and perhaps even the survival, of your organization (for-profit or not-for-profit), depends on having to do more with fewer resources. Many organizations—especially the people—find it necessary to reinvent themselves overnight, several times each year. Therefore, leaders of the third millennium must be creative and able to respond to the ever-changing demands of a volatile, rapidly-changing climate. Creative leadership is crucial to the short-term survivability and long-term success of each and every enterprise. Creative leadership is crucial to your personal effectiveness.

Perhaps you are thinking, like others, that "creative" is a trait reserved strictly for "artistic types," such as artists, musicians, writers, actors, and inventors. You may be thinking that the term "creative" is reserved for people who "ace" the SAT exam, or those who can speak several languages as a child, or those who "knock the top off" an IQ test. However, none of this is true. These are myths—each one of them. As Michael Michalko noted,

> (Creativity) is not about scoring 1600 on the SATs, mastering fourteen languages at the age of seven, finishing MENSA exercises in record time, having an extraordinarily high IQ, or even about being smart... creativity is not the same as intelligence. Any individual can be far more creative than he or she is intelligent. [34]

The truth of the matter is that you are creative. You were created to be creative. Creativity is an attribute given to each and every person—given to you—by God. Creativity is a crucial leadership trait. It is a trait that you must rediscover, claim, cultivate, and use in every dimension of your life. In doing so, you will be functioning as you were created to function, as a creative leader, as an image bearer of God. You have the very same creative capacity as Archimedes, King Gillette, Thomas Edison, or Bill Gates. You have the "right stuff" for leadership in the twenty-first century.

## Cultivating Creative Leadership

How, you may ask, do I cultivate this important leadership attribute? Rediscovering and cultivating this attribute, like all of your created attributes, will become a life-long pursuit. Stewarding this leadership trait will be a process. But if you don't begin today, you can't finish. Allow me to recommend five strategies for cultivating this important created leadership attribute.

First, as a starting point, complete the "Personal Reflection" exercise at the end of this chapter. As in previous chapters, don't rush this activity. Take time to reflect on each question before recording your responses.

Second, complete the "Cultivating Your Created Leadership Capacity" exercise, also found at the end of this chapter. This exercise will enable you to think through the important application of this leadership attribute in each one of your major life roles. Being creative is not some strange, new-age, or bizarre way of thinking. Though supernatural in origin, thinking creatively is actually a natural way of thinking. As Michalko observed:

> Creative thinking is the natural way to think, not a different way to think. We have been taught to think reproductively and logically and linearly. We have been told that 'creativity' itself must be taught and learned in the same fashion as other academic subjects. This is not so. [35]

Third, purchase and read a good book on living and thinking creatively. A brief search on the internet will lead you to several helpful books and articles. I found Michael Michalko's books to be readable, practical, and enormously useful: *Cracking Creativity: The Secrets of Creative Genius*.[36] I value Michalko's notion that each of us is creative, and that living creatively is the natural way to think. But I hasten to add, functioning creatively is also "natural" because God created you to be creative. It is God's nature. It is your created nature. I also recommend two other books by Michalko: *ThinkPad: A Brainstorming Card Deck*,[37] and *Tinkertoys: A Handbook of Business Creativity*.[38] One more time, let me remind you, leaders are readers!

Fourth, attend a seminar or special-topic course on creative thinking at one of your local colleges. Call each one of your local colleges and place your name and address on their mailing list. Look for advertisements in your local newspaper or brochures in your mail box. Call the area Chamber of Commerce to see what seminars on creativity will be offered in your community. Don't overlook the internet as a useful resource in locating helpful materials and workshops.

Fifth, and finally, there are a variety of creative tactics you can implement, beginning today, ranging from brainstorming activities to forming creativity committees in your home, church, work, and neighborhood. Following is an activity that you can begin and maintain on your own: start and keep a "Creativity Catalog." Today, on your way home from work, stop at the nearest office supply retailer and purchase a spiral bound notebook. I recommend one that is 8 ½ by 11 inches in size. If possible, find one that has two or three pocket files inside as well. Keep this notebook handy. Carry it with you throughout the day. Each and every day, like Archimedes, Antoine Feuchtwanger, King Gillette, and scores of others, you will have sudden flashes of inspiration about your personal life, family, church, and career. When this happens, take time to chronicle each creative idea in your "Creativity Catalog" or drop a handwritten note into one of the file pockets. From time to time, at least weekly, sit quietly and reflect on each and every creative idea you recorded in the "Creativity Catalog." Add more notes, ideas, and action steps that come to your mind as you review your creative thoughts and ideas. I will be so bold as to suggest that in a matter of a few weeks you will be implementing concrete action steps on at least one of the ideas recorded in your "Creativity Catalog." Make this practice part of your daily life—for the rest of your life. You will not run out of innovative ideas and creative solutions. Your life will become more fruitful, fulfilling, meaningful, and creative.

You are creative. You are a leader. This is the truth about leadership! This is the *Genesis Principle of Leadership*.

# Personal Reflection

### *Leaders are Creative*

- Leadership is reclaiming and cultivating your God-given, created attributes. What specific action steps will you take to develop this leadership trait: Creative?

- What does it mean that God is creative?

- List three ways in which God has been creative to you:

- List some specific actions you can take to be creative to others:

- Which action will you implement this week?

- To whom?

- What result(s) do you expect from taking this action?

- Take a few moments—now—to pray about this action.

- In what way(s) could you help someone in your family, workplace, or community to claim and cultivate this leadership attribute in his life?

- Cultivate this created leadership trait by completing the "Cultivating Your Created Leadership Capacity" exercise on the next page.

## Cultivating Your Created Leadership Capacity

Leadership is the lifelong pursuit of claiming and cultivating your God-created attributes.

1. Select a Life Role (e.g. Leader, Spouse, Parent, Worker, Neighbor, etc.).
2. List the key Duties and Responsibilities of that Life Role.
3. Then design and list specific Action Steps that will enable you to steward this leadership attribute.

## Cultivating Creative Leadership

As a leader you are imaginative, insightful, ingenious, inventive, and intentional enabling you to evaluate, comprehend, and generate creative ideas, resources, solutions, and transforming actions.

## Life Role:

_____

Duties/Responsibilities:   Leadership is Action:

1. _____ | _____
   _____ | _____
2. _____ | _____
   _____ | _____
3. _____ | _____
   _____ | _____
4. _____ | _____
   _____ | _____
5. _____ | _____
   _____ | _____
6. _____ | _____
   _____ | _____
7. _____ | _____
   _____ | _____

*What you do with what you know is what Christian knowing is all about.* (Os Guinness)

# Leaders Exercise Dominion

As a leader you possess the ability to purposefully exercise your inherent power and authority over that which is around you—which God created—as a responsible steward.

## A One-Woman World Power for Good

What names come to your mind when you think of "power:" Julius Caesar, Alexander the Great, Richard the Lionhearted? What about political leaders: George Washington, Abraham Lincoln, or Margaret Thatcher? What powerful business leaders come to mind: Lee Iacocca, Bill Gates? Then there are villainous leaders: Attila the Hun, Vladimir Lenin, Joseph Stalin, Adolph Hitler, or Osama bin Laden? Perhaps, like me, you think of powerful fictitious characters like Zeus, Luke Skywalker, James Bond, Superman, Batman, Spider Man, Wonder Woman, or Mighty Mouse. Though their motives differ, each character, real or fictional, conjures images of people who possess tremendous political, physical, mental, psychological, and personal power. They are rugged, good-looking, tall, wise, wealthy, strong, and powerful.

Not so for Agnes. Agnes Gonxhe Bojaxhiu possessed none of the characteristics normally associated with power and leadership: male, tall, strong, wealthy, and powerful. Quite the opposite; Agnes was female, small in stature, frail, poor, and lived most of her life in obscurity and anonymity. In fact, very little is known about her early life. We do know that she was born in 1910 in Yugoslavia (present day Macedonia), the youngest of three children born to Niholla and Dranafila. Her father was a successful building contractor. Agnes grew up in a predominantly Muslim community—quite a challenge for a family that was ethnically Albanian and religiously Catholic.

As early as the age of twelve, Agnes felt a vocational call to help the poor. This desire never left her. At age eighteen she joined the Sisters of Loreto, an Irish community of nuns. Following her training in Dublin, Agnes was sent to Darjeeling in India as a "novice sister." She made her first vows in 1931, choosing the name "Sister Mary Teresa." In 1937, she completed her vows, acquiring the title "Mother Teresa."

For over thirty years, Mother Teresa worked in relative obscurity teaching and working among the least of society. In 1950, she received permission to start her own religious order, "The Missionaries of Charity." Her mission was to care for the "poorest of the poor." Almost overnight, especially following the documentary "Something Beautiful for God" and the publication of her own book by that same title, Mother Teresa became an international celebrity. She received numerous awards, including the Nobel Peace Prize in 1979.

In spite of this notoriety, this small, frail, humble leader continued her work among the poor. She died in September 1997, at the age of eighty-seven. She left a rich legacy of leadership by serving the cause of the poor and dying. Today, The Missionaries of Charity is composed of over 4,000 sisters, a brotherhood of over 300 members, 10,000 volunteers, and 610 missions operating numerous hospices, homes, soup kitchens, orphanages, schools, and counseling centers in 123 countries including, intriguingly, the United States of America.

Little wonder that one journalist could say that Mother Teresa, Agnes Gonxhe Bojaxhiu, was "one frail nun who moved millions… a one-woman world power for good." At a full state funeral by the Indian government, U. N. Secretary General, Javier Perez de Cuellar, said, "She is the United Nations. She is the peace of the world." Agnes Gonxhe Bojaxhiu, Mother Teresa, was considered by many to be a mighty leader. Others called her a "superhero." On October 19, 2003, soon after her death (and amid some controversy), Pope John Paul II beatified Mother Teresa as "Blessed Teresa of Calcutta," the first major step toward canonization and possible sainthood.

## From Parenting to Presiding

Mother Teresa claimed and cultivated her inherent, God-given power and authority over that which was around her. She lived and labored amidst indescribable poverty, unimaginable disease, and gruesome death. Yet she was obedient to God's command to be fruitful, to fill the earth, and to subdue the earth by exercising dominion—even over a horrid situation. She obeyed God's command to exercise dominion using the very attribute God gave her when he created her. Or to put it another way, she emulated the characteristics given to all men and women as image bearers of God by exercising dominion (i.e. power) over every square inch of her corner of the world in Calcutta.

Effective leadership, the style of leadership that transforms people and circumstances, is ultimately the result of the proper use of this God-given attribute—power. Leaders possess, cultivate, and make use of their created power. Leadership is all about the exercise of power. As the Rt. Rev. Bennett J. Sims noted at the Annual Conference of the Institute for Servant Leadership on April 6, 2003 in Hendersonville, North Carolina: "From parenting to presiding... from the home to the White House... all leaders use power." Pittacus (c. 650—c. 570 BC), one of the seven wise men of ancient Greece, was correct when he said, "The measure of a man is what he does with power."

## The Source of All Power

The exercise of power is often misunderstood. Consequently, power is often misused and abused. History chronicles sordid accounts of men and women who abused their power with catastrophic consequences. Several important points must be understood about power. First, power can only be understood in the context of the power of God. God alone is all-powerful, that is, He alone is omnipotent. He is the source of power. All power and authority belong to God and to Him alone. God's power is inherent. That is, God did not acquire power. Nor is He subject to any power but His own. He is under no other being's power. No other being gave Him power. God's power is independent; it does not depend upon the recognition of any other being or authority. No person, no entity in the universe has any degree of power that does not come from the Author of power, God, the Creator. The Holy Scriptures are eminently clear about this:

> Once God has spoken; twice have I heard this: that power belongs to God (Psalm 62:11, ESV).

> Ascribe power to God, whose majesty is over Israel, and whose power is in the skies. Awesome is God from his sanctuary; the God of Israel—he is the one who gives power and strength to his people. Blessed be God! (Psalm 68:34–35, ESV).

O Lord God of hosts, who is mighty as you are, O Lord, with your faithfulness all around you? (Psalm 89:8, ESV).

Simply stated, there is no part of the universe that is not created by, owned by, and sustained by God's power. God's power cannot be checked, restrained, nor frustrated by any person, any thing, or any other power. As the famous theologian and "Prince of Preachers," Charles Haddon Spurgeon (1834–1892), observed:

> God's power is like Himself, self-existent and self-sustained. The mightiest of men cannot add so much as a shadow of power to the Omnipotent One. He sits on no buttressed throne and leans on no assisting air. His court is not maintained by His courtiers, nor does it honor its splendor from His creatures. God is Himself the great central source and Originator of all power. [39]

## Positional and Personal Power

Second, there are two kinds of power, positional power and personal power. Scripture identifies these as "*dunamis*" (Greek) and "*exousia*" (Greek). *Dunamis*, from which we derive the English word "dynamite," is positional power. Positional power is a form of power that is intrinsic to a particular position or title such as "Chief Executive Officer," "Supervisor," "Teacher," "Parent," "Ruling Elder," and others. Positional power is a form of power, or authority, over people, decision-making, scheduling, materials, supplies, money, and other resources that reside in one's position.

All men and women have positional power. God created mankind on the sixth day—a marvelous capstone to the act of creation. Consequently, you hold a unique position in God's creation. The Bible reveals that God created man just a little lower than the angels. Nonetheless, you are unique and superior to the rest of the creation. God not only created and appointed you to this distinctive position in the creation; He also gave you the ability—the power—to accomplish the specific task He assigned. You are the crown of creation. As such, you have been assigned control over the rest of creation. This control is described in Genesis 1:28. Here, all of humanity is commanded to "be fruitful and multiply and fill the earth and subdue it and have dominion over the fish of the sea and over the birds of the heavens and over every living thing that moves on the earth."

Some refer to this command as the "cultural mandate." I prefer Eugene Peterson's inimitably descriptive and more motivating term in *The Message, Genesis Charge.* You and I have been charged and equipped by God to responsibly exercise positional power in every arena of life. You may own businesses employing others. Perhaps you hold a managerial position in a for-profit or not-for-profit organization. Perhaps you are a civic leader, teacher, or volunteer. Perhaps, like many, you are a parent. In each and every instance, you have been given and are called to exercise your positional power in each particular life role and calling.

You also possess "*exousia.*" *Exousia* is personal power. Personal power is not linked to your title or position. Personal power is your ability to effectively exercise influence over people far beyond your natural skills and abilities—a type of divine enablement that compels others to join in the cause—to follow the flag. What set of character traits and qualities account for personal power? As you might expect, some suggest that the genetic code explains personal power. Some have it—others don't. Others argue that personal power is the consequence of growing up in the "right" environment. Still others suggest that personal power is strictly "granted" by the followers. None of this is true. Personal power emanates from within those who reclaim and cultivate their God-given capacity to exercise dominion.

## Using Your Created Power

Third, you are to employ your created power. Not only has God commanded you to exercise dominion, He has given you the capacity to fulfill His *Genesis Charge*. He has given you the ability to reclaim and cultivate your inherent positional and personal power. Therefore, you are to avail yourself of these created "powers" in every arena of your life, as head of your household, as parent to your children, as a member of your church, as a leader in your community and country, and in your position in your workplace. Genesis 1:28 is a directive from God. You will be held responsible for how you respond to His personal charge. You will be asked to give an account for just how well you reclaimed, cultivated, and stewarded the positional and personal power God entrusted to you in your various life roles. When this power is used properly, it injects a sense of excellence into even the most mundane positional task. This excellence will then produce in you a sense of God's delight and glory, no matter your calling or responsibilities. As Martin Luther King, Jr. once said:

> All labor...should be carried out with painstaking excellence. If a man discovers that he is called to be a street sweeper, he should seek to sweep streets like Michelangelo painted pictures, like Beethoven composed music, and like Shakespeare wrote poetry. He should sweep streets so well that all the host of heaven and earth will have to pause and say "here lived a great street sweeper who swept his job well."[40]

## Deep-Spirited Leadership

Peculiar as it may seem at first, when you rightly rediscover, cultivate, and utilize your positional and personal power, you actually make others more powerful. You enable others to rediscover, cultivate, and call forth their positional and personal power (along with all the other created attributes) God has given to them. You enable others to make a difference in their individual circumstances and to make a difference in their spheres of influence. This is not "empowering" (as some misapply this overused, abusive, and crippling term). Empowering, as it is popularly used today, implies that you are going to equip others with something they do not possess. Rather, "empowering" in this sense means that you are going to use your created capacity to call forth the same created capacity in others—attributes already given to them by God. Collectively, this God-given power will turn an upside down world right side up!

A distinctive feature of effective leadership is the intentional ability to call forth the created attributes, skills, aspirations, and gifts of those about them. True leaders are not threatened or intimidated by the strengths of others. As odd as it may sound, leaders prefer to surround themselves with people who are stronger and more capable than themselves. What's more, leaders invest personal time in mentoring, developing, and encouraging others to become even stronger. Outstanding leaders practice what I call "Philippian Leadership." That is, leaders do nothing from rivalry or self-centeredness. Rather, in humility leaders regard others more significant than themselves. They do not look at just their own interests, but to the interests of others (Philippians 2:3–4). Eugene Peterson, author and translator of *The Message*, captured the essence of this important leadership characteristic in Philippians 2:3–7:

Don't push your way to the front; don't sweet-talk your way to the top. Put yourself aside, and help others get ahead. Don't be obsessed with getting your own advantage. Forget yourselves long enough to lend a helping hand. Think of yourselves the way Christ Jesus thought of himself. He had equal status with God but didn't think so much of himself that he had to cling to the advantages of that status no matter what. Not at all. When the time came, he set aside the privileges of deity and took on the status of a slave, became human! Having become human, he stayed human. It was an incredibly humbling process. He didn't claim special privileges.

This is "deep-spirited" leadership! This is how the redemption of the long-lost attributes of God takes place! This is how the redemption of the world catches fire and spreads!

## Beware of Throwing Rocks

Fourth, take heed to what can happen if you are disobedient to the *Genesis Charge*. Beware of the consequences when you choose not to reclaim and cultivate the power (positional and personal) given to you by God. God created you with the capability to exercise dominion—to responsibly use your positional and personal power to redeem every corner of the creation. This is God's command. You cannot and must not avoid this responsibility. If you fail to rediscover, cultivate, and utilize this created attribute, it allows others, often power-hungry and villainous people, to fill the void created by your disobedience. Over time you will completely lose power and authority over your family, school, government, judicial systems, and churches. You will lose the ability to lead others in the discovery and cultivation of their positional and personal power. This ultimately leads to the destruction of the individual and the decay of the world.

For example, I join millions of people across our nation who are gravely concerned about the state of public education. Frankly, it is rather easy—even delightful at times—to stand on the sidelines with my bag of rocks throwing them at the school officials for the sad state of the public school systems. However, and I am deeply remorseful about this, I should be throwing stones at myself for allowing the public schools to have deteriorated to such a deplorable condition. In the final analysis it is us Christians that are responsible for allowing the schools to slip through our fingers. We are the ones who stood by and allowed the decay to occur.

## "The Measure of a Man Is What He Does With Power"

I encourage you to initiate two simple strategies that will help you to cultivate this important leadership trait. First, complete the "Personal Reflection" exercise at the end of this chapter. Take time to thoughtfully and intentionally reflect on each question before recording your responses. By now these questions are familiar to you—but invest quality time in responding to each one.

Second, complete the "Cultivating Your Created Leadership Capacity" exercise, also found at the end of this chapter. This exercise will help you think through how best to apply your created leadership power in each one of your major life roles and spheres of influence. Remember, like God, you have the ability to purposefully exercise your inherent power and authority over that which is around you—which God created—as a responsible steward. Claim and cultivate this attribute for yourself. You are to exercise power because God created and charged you to exercise power. Pittacus, one of the seven sages of ancient Greece, had it right—"The measure of a man is what he does with power."

You are to exercise dominion. You are a leader. This is the truth about leadership! This is the *Genesis Principle of Leadership*.

# Personal Reflection

### *Leaders Exercise Power*

- Leadership is reclaiming and cultivating your God-given, created attributes. What specific action steps will you take to develop this leadership trait: *Exercise Power?*

- What does it mean that God exercises power?

- List three ways in which God exercised power to you:

- List some specific actions you can take to exercise power to others:

- Which action will you implement this week?

- To whom?

- What result(s) do you expect from taking this action?

- Take a few moments—now—to pray about this action.

- In what way(s) could you help someone in your family, workplace, or community to claim and cultivate this leadership attribute in his life?

- Cultivate this created leadership trait by completing the "Cultivating Your Created Leadership Capacity" exercise on the next page.

## Cultivating Your Created Leadership Capacity

Leadership is the lifelong pursuit of claiming and cultivating your God-created attributes.

1. Select a Life Role (e.g. Leader, Spouse, Parent, Worker, Neighbor, etc.).

2. List the key Duties and Responsibilities of that Life Role.

3. Then design and list specific Action Steps that will enable you to steward this leadership attribute.

## Cultivating Powerful Leadership

As a leader you possess the ability to purposefully exercise your inherent power and authority over that which is around you—which God created—as a responsible steward.

## Life Role:

_____

| Duties/Responsibilities: | Leadership is Action: |
|---|---|
| 1. | |
| 2. | |
| 3. | |
| 4. | |
| 5. | |
| 6. | |
| 7. | |

*What you do with what you know is what Christian knowing is all about.* (Os Guinness)

# Leaders Are Moral

As a leader you are capable of thoughts and actions that have principled qualities. Hence your interactions and dealings with others can be properly designated as "right" or "wrong."

## Character Matters

"If you're gonna kill a guy like LeMessurier, why should anyone ever talk?"

Imagine that you are the world's most famous structural engineer. You've achieved international fame and fortune. You've received numerous honors for your innovative designs of some of the tallest buildings in the world. Clients from around the globe are standing in line for your designs. Suddenly you are confronted with an engineer's worst nightmare. Under certain wind conditions, your building might collapse, killing or maiming thousands of people. Your personal and professional reputation would be ruined by such a catastrophic calamity. So what would you do? Remain silent? Lie? Commit suicide?

Really, what would *you* do? For you see, moral character matters. Moral character makes a difference in the executive suites of the corporate world, in pastors' studies, and in your personal and professional dealings with others. Nearly every day, the news headlines reflect the elements of a Greek tragedy as they chronicle the tragic, heartrending, usually shameful and reprehensible accounts of men and women who disregarded a simple truth—morality matters.

Morality mattered for structural engineer William LeMessurier. LeMessurier had received numerous honors and recognitions for his innovative designs and extensive experience building mammoth skyscrapers. He was elected into the prestigious National Academy of Engineers for his outstanding achievements. He designed several famous structures, including Boston's State Street Bank, the Boston Federal Reserve Bank, and the Citicorp Center, one of the tallest buildings in midtown Manhattan. On the website, *TheCityReview.com*,[41] Carter Horsley described the Citicorp Center as "soaring," "sleek," "the most dramatic skyscraper to be erected in Midtown since the Chrysler Building," and "one of the most daring designs to be completed in the city's history." Peculiar to this fifty-nine-story, 915.4 foot tall structure is the presence of St. Peter's Lutheran Church, located on the patio just outside of this visually stunning edifice.

Just one year after the completion of the Citicorp Center, LeMessurier was staggered to learn that the building that had earned him international acclaim had an Achilles' heel. He received a phone call from an engineering student, whose name has since been forgotten, who felt that under certain wind conditions, LeMessurier's fifty-nine-story architectural masterpiece might collapse. This staggering revelation was LeMessurier's worst nightmare. The structural integrity of his building was destroyed. LeMessurier was astounded, flabbergasted, to learn that during construction a crucial change had been made, without his knowledge or approval, in the way in which the joints of the building were braced together. Instead of welding the joints of this massive steel structure as he detailed in his engineering specifications, contractors chose to bolt the joints together. This left the building unnecessarily sensitive to certain kinds of winds known as "quartering winds." What's more, the substituted bolts had been under-designed. The odds for a devastating catastrophe were appalling. It was calculated that the seventh tallest building in the world had a one in sixteen chance of collapsing if hit by quartering winds from a hurricane, an event that occurred in Manhattan once every sixteen years. To make matters worse, the hurricane season was approaching. Furthermore, there had not been a strong hurricane in Manhattan for several years. Would this be the year?

## "There's No Other Choice to Make"

Dazed by this shocking revelation, LeMessurier retreated to his remote summer home to consider his options. Silence was one option. Perhaps nothing would happen and no one would ever know of the weakness hidden in the structure of this magnificent showpiece. By not saying anything he might preserve his reputation and fortune. Suicide was yet another option. But this would only be a cowardly way out and put thousands of other lives at risk.

Then it occurred to him. He possessed knowledge that nobody else in the world had. This made him feel extraordinarily powerful. He knew what he had to do. He had to blow the whistle on himself. At risk was personal humiliation and professional embarrassment. Looking back at this decision, LeMessurier felt almost giddy with the power he held in his hands to affect extraordinary events that only he could initiate. LeMessurier said to himself, "Thank you, dear Lord, for making this problem so sharply defined that there's no other choice to make."

So he did just that. LeMessurier blew the whistle on himself. With his illustrious career and personal wealth hanging in the balance, LeMessurier met with Citicorp's chairman, Walter B. Wriston, saying, "I have a real problem for you, sir." But LeMessurier also offered a workable solution. Within minutes everyone pulled out their yellow legal pads and outlined a comprehensive strategy including press releases, emergency contingency plans, and the work needed to repair the problem.

LeMessurier did not know how this news would be received. He feared that the revelation of the building's vulnerability would drive a nail in the coffin of his distinguished reputation as the world's premier structural engineer. Much to his surprise and relief, he was commended for his courage, integrity, and moral character. Energy was not wasted placing blame. No one wanted to hang him. As the mayor of the city stated,

> It started with a guy who stood up and said, "I got a problem, I made the problem, let's fix the problem." If you're gonna kill a guy like LeMessurier, why should anyone ever talk?

The problem was fixed. Today the Citicorp Center far exceeds its originally intended safety margins. Astonishingly, LeMessurier's reputation increased as one of the most competent, forthright, and honest structural engineers in the world. LeMessurier's liability insurer even lowered his annual premium because of his integrity. LeMessurier did the right thing. Morality mattered. Thousands of lives were saved.

## Reason Deceives—Conscience Never

Where does moral character come from? Does it result from one's genetic code? Is morality acquired from the environment? Is it a product of evolution? Or is morality the result of a social contract? Actually, morality is none of these things. Morality finds its origin in God. By nature, God is a moral agent. He always does what is right. When we say, "God is moral," we are saying that God does what He does because it is, in reality, moral. He is the emphasis and perfection of integrity and righteousness. In the final analysis, He is the absolute standard and source of what is right and good.

As the standard and source of morality, God created you to be a moral agent. Therefore, you were created to conform to God's perfect moral standard in thought, word, and deed. This demand and desire is folded into the fabric of who you are as a human. It is who you were designed to be. As Pope Paul VI inculcated,

> Deep within their consciences men and women discover a law which they do not lay upon themselves, and which they must obey. Its voice, ever calling them to love and to do what is good and to avoid evil, tells them inwardly at the right moment: to do this, shun that. For they have in their hearts a law inscribed by God. Their dignity rests in observing this law, and by it they will be judged.[42]

Or as the Apostle Paul instructed, all men and women have the law of God (His perfect standard for what is right and what is wrong) written on their hearts:

> They show that the work of the law is written on their hearts, while their conscience also bears witness, and their conflicting thoughts accuse or even excuse them…
>
> Romans 2:15 (ESV)

As a created moral agent, you are capable of thoughts and actions that have principled qualities. Your interactions and dealings with others can be properly designated as "right" or "wrong." It is your moral duty to follow and obey your moral conscience—to do, always, what you know, deep down inside, is the absolute right thing to do.

## First, the Bad News

There is a problem, however. Man's rebellion against God's standard for morality distorted the attributes of God you were created to emulate. You were made to follow the voice of God calling you to love and do what is good and to avoid evil. But sin brutally damaged your righteous and moral dealings with others. As Jean Jacques Rousseau summarized it, "Reason deceives; conscience, never."[43]

## Then, the Good News!

Though this attribute has been greatly obscured by sin, you still possess and must act upon your innate sense of right and wrong. This sense of right and wrong, given when you were created, is commonly called "conscience." Your conscience is so deeply rooted in the core of your personhood that you hardly recognize its existence. However, make no mistake about it; your conscience is not the product of genetic coding. Your conscience is not the product of external influences exerted upon you by the environment (e.g. a mother adept at using guilt as a weapon to force her opinion). Conscience is the consequence of being made in the image of a moral God. In the creation God chiseled His standard for right and wrong, good and evil, onto your soul. Therefore, you cannot plead ignorance of your particular moral obligations. For example, everyone knows it is wrong to kick puppies. And no one would applaud a man for declaring absolute fidelity to his wife, all the while keeping seven other wives in seven other cities. Your conscience is proof that God's standard for morality is part of who you are. It is for this reason that God will hold you accountable for how well (or poorly) you did what was clearly right.

## Doing What is Right

So, what *is* right? What standard serves as the reliable basis for informing your conscience? Is there a standard independent of personal beliefs and individual convictions? The conventional wisdom of today's culture demands that there is no independent, absolute standard by which you can discern what is "right" or "wrong" in every situation. You are to do what *you* deem is the most appropriate action demanded in each unique situation. It is a matter of "personal choice." What is "right" or "wrong" for one person may not be "right" or "wrong" for another. Moral standards, then, are relative. What's more, there is no autonomous basis by which to judge another's conscience, standards, or actions. Each person must choose for himself the rightness or wrongness of a particular action.

Before mankind's fall into sin, it was sufficient for God to have implanted His moral law into the human heart. It was enough for man to follow his bare conscience. However, in a fallen condition, man's conscience is inadequate and untrustworthy. Mankind, you and I, is no longer capable of determining and doing what is right in every life circumstance. Therefore, God was pleased to provide a clear revelation of His moral law in the Holy Scriptures—His inspired, infallible, reliable, and written word. This Word reveals God's moral standard and will for all of faith and life. Through this word, you can know, utterly and completely, independently of your sin-distorted conscience, what is, in fact, the right thing to do in every circumstance of life. God's Word, the Bible, is the moral standard given to govern your character. The Holy Scripture is the completely sufficient rule for your faith and daily living. It is the external, absolute, and trustworthy standard created by the perfectly moral God. By it you may know what is right. Without reading the Holy Scripture in its entirety, you have no way of knowing and applying these standards to the circumstances of your life.

The One who created you in His image, the One who created you as a moral agent, expects you to act in accordance with His moral standards. He has recorded these standards in His own Word, the Holy Bible. These scriptures leave no guess work as to what God expects from you. The Bible was written for you to read, learn, and apply to your life. So, the first step in cultivating this God-given attribute is to read, study, and apply God's written word. It is your moral obligation to obey your biblically-informed conscience, doing what God said is *the* right thing to do.

For some, the "Ten Commandments" (Deuteronomy 5:6–21, ESV) are the best summary of God's moral will for us:

- "You shall have no other gods before me."

- "You shall not take the name of the Lord your God in vain."

- "Observe the Sabbath day, to keep it holy, as the Lord your God commanded you."

- "Honor your father and your mother."

- "You shall not murder."

- "And you shall not commit adultery."

- "And you shall not steal."

- "And you shall not bear false witness against your neighbor."

- "And you shall not covet your neighbor's wife."

- "And you shall not desire your neighbor's house, his field, or his male servant, or his ox, or his donkey, or anything that is your neighbor's."

Others advocate Psalm 15 as an excellent summary of God's moral will. Others have adopted the Beatitudes from Jesus' Sermon on the Mount found in Matthew 5. Some suggest the well-known "Golden Rule" found in Matthew 7:12 as the best moral guide: "So whatever you wish that others would do to you do also to them, for this is the Law and the Prophets" (ESV).

I prefer Jesus' summary of God's moral law. When the Pharisees asked, "Teacher, which is the greatest commandment in the law?" (Matthew 22:36, ESV). Jesus answered,

> You shall love the Lord your God with all your heart and with all your soul and with all your mind. This is the great and first commandment. And a second is like it: You shall love your neighbor as yourself. On these two commandments depend all the Law and the Prophets.
>
> Matthew 22:37–40 (ESV)

The point is this: morality, your morality, is not formed in a relativistic vacuum. God not only created you as a moral agent, He provided the moral standard by which you can judge the nature of every one of your thoughts and actions. You either trust in God and His moral standards or you are left to trust in your own unbelief. To attempt to make moral choices outside of God's moral standards is fool hearty and utterly irresponsible. God's

Word is the fixed point from which every one of your thoughts and actions will be judged by the Author of the standards.

Choosing the right and proper thing to do regarding whom to marry, stances on current social and political issues, lifestyle, and career paths can be very difficult and distressing, especially in a diverse and pluralistic culture that is constantly pushing the notion that "anything goes." It requires that you reclaim and cultivate the very attribute that God created that will enable you to discern and act appropriately in every life circumstance. This will require a lifetime of work. But through this work you can fulfill God's will in and through your life.

## Morality Matters

Effective leaders are moral agents. In other words, leaders do the right things. Leaders cultivate this key leadership attribute by identifying and developing a set of biblically-principled core standards by which they conduct their actions in every leadership role. But these standards are not drawn from the "moral cafeteria" of the culture. Truly effective leaders recognize there are standards of conduct that are completely independent of mere human choice. As the self-made billionaire, Jon Huntsman, put it, "There should not be tension between making profits and adhering to traditional principles of fairness and decency."[44]

You are a moral agent. Your thoughts and actions are not the reflexive and habitual consequences of the surrounding environment. Your thoughts and actions are not instinctive reactions driven by the genetic code. Yes, genetics and the press of the environment influence and impact you. But as a moral agent, you have moral reasons for each of your actions. A fruitful and fulfilling life is a life lived morally. Morality matters.

## Cultivating Moral Leadership

I encourage you to initiate two additional action steps that will enable you to cultivate this important leadership trait. First, complete the "Personal Reflection" exercise at the end of this chapter. Take time to thoughtfully and intentionally reflect on each question before recording your responses. Continue to invest quality time in responding to each question.

Second, complete the "Cultivating Your Created Leadership Capacity" exercise, also found at the end of this chapter. This exercise will help you think through how best to apply moral leadership in each one of your major life roles and spheres of influence. Remember, like God, you are capable of thoughts and actions that have principled qualities. Hence your interactions with others can be properly evaluated as "right" or "wrong." Claim and cultivate this attribute.

You are moral. You are a leader. This is the truth about leadership! This is the *Genesis Principle of Leadership*.

# Personal Reflection

## *Leaders Are Moral*

- Leadership is reclaiming and cultivating your God-given, created attributes. What specific action steps will you take to develop this leadership trait: *Moral?*

- What does it mean that God is moral?

- List three ways in which God has been moral to you:

- List some specific actions you can take to be moral to others:

- Which action will you implement this week?

- To whom?

- What result(s) do you expect from taking this action?

- Take a few moments—now—to pray about this action.

- In what way(s) could you help someone in your family, workplace, or community to claim and cultivate this leadership attribute in his life?

- Cultivate this created leadership trait by completing the "Cultivating Your Leadership Attributes" exercise on the next page.

## Cultivating Your Created Leadership Capacity

Leadership is the lifelong pursuit of claiming and cultivating your God-created attributes.

1. Select a *Life Role* (e.g. *Leader, Spouse, Parent, Worker, Neighbor,* etc.).
2. List the key *Duties and Responsibilities* of that *Life Role.*
3. Then design and list specific *Action Steps* that will enable you to steward this leadership attribute.

## Cultivating Moral Leadership

As a leader you are capable of thoughts and actions that have principled qualities. Hence, your interactions and dealings with others can be properly designated as "right" or "wrong."

## Life Role:

_____

| Duties/Responsibilities: | Leadership is Action: |
|---|---|
| 1. _____ | _____ |
| 2. _____ | _____ |
| 3. _____ | _____ |
| 4. _____ | _____ |
| 5. _____ | _____ |
| 6. _____ | _____ |
| 7. _____ | _____ |

*What you do with what you know is what Christian knowing is all about.* (Os Guinness)

# Leaders Are Relational

As a leader you are capable of developing intentional and interpersonal relationships, emphasizing high regard for the well-being and personhood of others.

## Better Together

I love the seasonal changes. I live in a part of the United States where the changing of the seasons is prolonged and unhurried, adding to my pleasure and enjoyment of each one. Each season is unique, extraordinary, and thrilling. I must admit, though, that fall is my favorite season. I enjoy the cool, crisp, dry air; the brilliant colors of the trees; the deep blue clear sky; and, the pungent smell of burning leaves.

One of the most enjoyable experiences of the fall season is watching large flocks of Canadian geese flying in their distinctive V-formations as they make their annual pilgrimage southward. There is so much to be learned by watching these magnificent birds. For example, scientists have observed that by flying in a tight V-formation, each bird creates a draft that reduces the wind resistance for the bird flying behind. The net effect is that the flying range for the flock is over seventy percent greater than if each bird flew solo. It's interesting to watch the geese take turns flying as the lead goose. As a result, no goose gets too tired, which would slow down the flight, endangering the entire flock. I also enjoy hearing the distinctive honking of the geese as they fly overhead. This honking also serves a good purpose. Honking encourages the lead goose to keep up air speed. And, curiously, if a goose gets sick or falls because it is wounded by a hunter, two or three geese will follow the injured goose to the ground and stay with it until it is able to fly or dies. Then they will join another passing flock and continue their journey southward.

What a marvelous example of what can be accomplished when people live and work together. I have a colorfully framed poster hanging in my office that powerfully summarizes the important leadership principle learned from observing migrating geese: "None of us is as good as all of us!" I'm sure you've heard similar statements such as:

Two heads are better than one.

Alone we can do so little, together we can do so much.

Never doubt that a small group of thoughtful people can change the world; indeed it is the only thing that ever has.

There is an Ethiopian proverb that puts it this way: "Many spider webs can hold down a lion." John Heywood, the English dramatist of the sixteenth century, famous for having said, "Rome was not built in a day," is the one who also said, "Many hands make light work." The slogan at Harvard University's Kennedy School of Government says it best, "Better Together."

Each slogan is an important reminder of the indispensability of teamwork and the strength of living and working together.

## Solo Sapiens

Sadly, however, people seem to have lost sight of this important leadership principle. In his groundbreaking, best-selling book, *Bowling Alone: The Collapse and Revival of American Community*, Robert Putnam[45] warned of the collapse of the vital communal characteristics in our culture. He argued that we have become relationally disconnected from family, friends, neighbors, and our societal structures such as school, work, church, community organizations, and others. Putnam noted that we sign fewer petitions, belong to fewer clubs and organizations, volunteer less, know our neighbors less, and spend less time with our families and friends. He added that more Americans are bowling than ever before, but they are "bowling alone." Consequently, our personal lives and our communities are impoverished.

Putnam worried that this social disengagement and alienation over the past thirty-five years is destroying social trust in our culture. It is this social trust that was described by Alexis de Tocqueville as the most distinguishing element of America's democratic greatness and heritage. As Tocqueville observed, "Nothing, in my view, deserved more attention than the intellectual and moral associations in America."[46] Putnam observed that children today are unhappy, teachers are afraid of their students, crime is increasing, and we distrust our neighbors. All this, according to Putnam, is because of the recent and rapid decline of the social capital that, according to de Tocqueville, made America great. One of my friends and colleagues, a clinical psychologist, told me that loneliness is the single biggest malady among his clients.

## It Doesn't Have To Be Like This

You are inherently relational. You were created by God for intentional and deeply interpersonal relationships. Your personhood and calling as a bearer of God's image is to be expressed and fleshed out in community. Such communal living requires the unconditional commitment of your time, talent, and treasure, together with a high regard for the well-being and personhood of others. Put more simply, you were not made to live as a solo sapien. It is not good for men and women—you—to be alone.

A healthy life is one filled with intentional relationships. Indeed, opportunities for purposeful relationships surround you. You have a relationship with God; you have a relationship with yourself; and you have a variety of relationships with other people, superiors, subordinates, co-workers, clients, family members, church members, neighbors, grocery store clerks, the mail carrier, and scores of others. The trouble is that too many people are failing to take advantage of these abundant relational opportunities.

Leaders embrace the indispensability of relationships. Effective leadership is built upon and depends on relationships. Through effective leadership you seek to influence the ideas, beliefs, conduct, and activities of others moving them together toward common goals and objectives.

## A Classic Model

Nowhere is this relational model of leadership more evident than in the three distinctive persons of the Godhead. God the Father, God the Son, and God the Holy Spirit live in an eternal and familial relationship. Their desire and ability to live intentionally with each other has always been, and forever will be, from eternity to eternity, part of the very essence of God. God is relational. God is familial in His character. God exists in community.

The loving community of the three-personal God has been depicted in a variety of symbolic ways: three intertwined and overlapping circles, a flower with just three petals, or a triangle enclosed in a circle. Each symbol attempts to depict one of the great, yet mysterious, truths of the Bible—God is three in one—living eternally in a deeply interpersonal and intentional relationship. The Godhead is the perfect model for establishing and developing proper functioning relationships and for the impact that relational leadership can have on your relationships.

As you develop and grow into the leader God designed you to be, it is important to realize that just as the triune God is by nature relational, so too, you are relational by your created nature. You were created to exist within the context of relationships; relationships that reflect the relationship between the three persons of the Trinity. In other words, because God is a social being, He created you to be a social being. Like God, you are to live relationally in every arena of your life (home, work, church, school, and community). This reality is the key to unlocking a life of fruitfulness and fulfillment. As Leroy Howe noted,

> Human beings are created for community and nothing accomplished by way of individual fulfillment and aggrandizement can fully compensate us for the misery suffered when the supportive structures of genuine community are compromised. [47]

## Living and Leading Relationally

There are three distinguishing characteristics of relational leadership. First, this created attribute is an interpersonal enterprise that begins with knowing and loving God; second, relational leadership expands by knowing and loving others; and, relational leadership is completed by knowing and loving yourself. Living relationally begins with knowing and loving God. As Jesus commanded,

> You shall love the Lord your God with all your heart and with all your soul and with all your mind. This is the great and first commandment. And the second is like it: You shall love your neighbor as yourself. On these two commandments depend the Law and the Prophets.
>
> Matthew 22:37–40 (ESV)

Pay particular attention to the priorities ordered in this passage. It is not unimportant. First and foremost, you are to intentionally pursue a relationship with God. This is the first thing God expects from you. It is the very first thing you must focus upon. You are, as Jesus instructed, to love God with every fiber of your being—with all your heart, with all your soul, and with all your intellect.

This individual and purposeful relationship with God is the beginning of effective leadership. It is the single most important relationship you have. Every other relationship, personal and professional, springs from your relationship to God. Without establishing and nurturing your relationship with God, all other relationships will be fruitless, unfulfilling, and empty.

But just how are you supposed to love God? You love God by glorifying and enjoying Him. And how do you glorify Him? You glorify and enjoy Him by loving God and keeping His commands. And where do you learn how to love and obey God? You learn how to love God in God's own Word, the Bible. The Bible shows you how to foster a relationship with the Creator. In other words, it shows you how to love God by reveling in the glory of

His character, the perfection of His justice, and the depth of His love for you.

Clearly, this is not an original idea. *The Westminster Shorter Catechism,* a document drafted by a group of pastors and theologians in the seventeenth century as a summary of the Bible's teachings, declares this same truth. The second question of the *Catechism* asks, "What rule hath God given to direct us how we may glorify and enjoy Him?" The answer to this question instructs that "The word of God, which is contained in the Scriptures of the Old and New Testaments, is the only rule to direct us how we may glorify and enjoy him." The *Catechism* continues by asking a related question, "What do the Scriptures principally teach?" The answer to this question expands our understanding of how to glorify and enjoy God, "The Scriptures principally teach what man is to believe concerning God, and what duty God requires of man."[48]

In other words, the Bible, the Word of God written, is God's rule—and the only rule—given to direct you how to glorify and enjoy Him. In short, you come to know, glorify, enjoy, and love God by reading His Word. In the Bible, you learn about and nurture a personal relationship with God. You comprehend His perfect holiness by learning the equity of His judgments and by being confronted with His love. In the Bible God reveals Himself, yourself, and His plans and purposes for your life. This is how you learn to glorify God and to enjoy Him forever.

What's the implication of this reality? Simply stated, begin—today—the practice of reading the Bible on a regular and systematic basis. In the Bible, by the divine enablement of God the Holy Spirit, you will learn about the basis of your love and enjoyment of God as the Father's grace is revealed through the living Word, Jesus Christ, God the Son. As one of my colleagues says, "The Bible is the best leadership textbook I know."

## "Bankrupt Without Love"

Next, relational leadership develops when you pursue your obligation to know and love your neighbor as yourself. This, too, is ordered in the Bible. You are to recognize that each and every person you encounter is created, like yourself, in the image of God. Every person is a product of God's workmanship deserving honor, esteem, and high regard. You are, in fact, to regard others as more important than you regard yourself. "Do nothing from rivalry or conceit, but in humility count others more significant than yourselves" (Philippians 2:3, ESV). Or as the Puritan, Matthew Henry put it in his commentary on Matthew 22:37–40:

> We must honour and esteem all men, and must wrong and injure no one; we must have good will to all, and good wishes for all, and, as we have opportunity, must do good to all … we must deny ourselves for the good of our neighbor, and must make ourselves servants to the full welfare of others … to lay down our lives for the brethren. [49]

If you are not willing to make yourself a servant to the full welfare of others, if you are not willing to lay down your life for others, then everything you do amounts to nothing. If you do not have love, you are nothing, you have nothing, and you gain nothing. Eugene Peterson put it this way in his translation of the Bible, *The Message* (I Corinthians 13: 1–3):

> If I speak with human eloquence and angelic ecstasy but don't love, I'm nothing but the creaking of a rusty gate. If I speak God's Word with power, revealing all his mysteries and making everything plain as day, and if I have faith that says to a mountain, "Jump," and it jumps, but I don't love,

I'm nothing. If I give everything I own to the poor and even go to the stake to be burned as a martyr, but I don't love, I've gotten nowhere. So, no matter what I say, what I believe, and what I do, I'm bankrupt without love.

Leadership is the process of influencing others by fostering appropriate and desired behavior while moving toward a defined goal. This cannot occur unless you work at building positive and effective relationships with the people you are leading. Leadership cannot take place in isolation. Therefore, you must understand people to lead people. Understanding people begins by developing a genuine concern and respect for them. This is why building and developing personal communication and relationship skills is crucial to becoming an effective leader.

There are a variety of simple and inexpensive ways by which you can intentionally grow and develop your relational leadership capacity. Here are just a few simple but effective ideas to get you started. I know you can add others to this list:

- Mentor a new employee
- Organize a company sports team
- Attend home parties when invited
- Ask co-workers and employees for their help and advice—and reciprocate
- Attend a seminar on team building
- Say "hello" to your employees and co-workers
- Host a cookout at your home for your employees
- Get to know something about all your employees

- Encourage your employees to host community group meetings on your site
- Eat lunch in the break room
- Eat breakfast with your employees
- Roll up your sleeves and work alongside your employees from time to time.
- Attend sporting events with your employees
- Share produce from your garden
- Host and attend monthly potluck lunches
- Attend in-house seminars with your employees
- Acknowledge and recognize special accomplishments and achievements
- Organize and participate in a fitness program with co-workers and employees
- Ask to see family photos of your co-workers
- Attend weddings, baptisms, and funerals
- Now, add a few of your own ideas to this list:

## Know Thyself

Finally, relational leadership is completed by loving yourself. I am not speaking about a form of love that is selfish, corrupt, and at the expense of others. Since man's fall into sin, everyone has been plagued with certain fundamental questions about their existence: Who am I? How did I get here? Why am I here?

Where am I headed? Where will I end up? What will happen to me after I die? Thales (546–640), an eminent Greek philosopher and scientist, grappled with the same questions and concluded, "Know thyself." As another mystic asked,

> What do you seek, O Pilgrim on the path? Liberation from pain and freedom from all suffering? The answer to thy quest is already in the heart. Listen, O Pilgrim, to the whispering of the soul. Know thyself, for in thyself is found all there is to be known.

Develop a humble, respectful, and biblical view of yourself as a special creation—carefully and wonderfully made—in the very image of the Creator Himself—with a unique body, distinctive gifts, exceptional talents, and extraordinary abilities. All interactions with your family, friends, and co-workers, no matter how well intended, will be empty and meaningless without a proper view (holy and wholly) of yourself. Without knowing and loving yourself, it will be impossible for you to develop a proper view of others. Your view and love for self and others as made in God's image must be preserved and sanctified. As Jesus said, all of life—body, soul, and spirit—hang on this reality.

As a member of a family, workgroup, church, or community organization, you are relational. You share a common understanding and commitment to the preferred future of the group, that is, its vision. You share a common understanding of and fundamental commitment to why the group exists, that is, its mission. Members of the group strive together to make a difference, to leave an indelible mark in the tapestry of life and the chronicles of mankind. You share a set of core values, a set of standards by which the group conducts its mission and vision. You are relational because God created you to be so. People are better together. You do need each other—not in a self-serving or co-dependent manner—but because God created people this way. You become all you can be by reclaiming and cultivating this vitally important created attribute.

Every person is created in the image of God. Every person shares equally the same created attributes and shares an equal responsibility as bearers of God's image to use these attributes in every aspect of life for mutual and corporate benefit. You are, in fact, to help others steward these attributes.

## Fostering a Culture of Forgiveness

The final feature of relational leadership is that it is intentional. Living and working effectively doesn't just happen simply because people were given the relational attribute in the creation. Living and working relationally is hard work. Remember, this attribute, like all the other created attributes, was terribly distorted by sin. Cultivating relational leadership requires effort, time, patience, and, from time to time, forgiveness. Taking risks is daily fare. This dramatically increases the opportunities for unresolved conflict and human failures. Consequently, relational leadership that is intentional requires leaders to exercise forgiveness. Yet, very few leadership books even mention the importance of exercising forgiveness. The consequences are often disastrous. Learning to practice forgiveness is essential to effective relational leadership.

In their book, *Leaders*, Warren Bennis and Burt Nanus[50] tell the inspiring story of a young, bright, junior executive at IBM who made a ten million dollar mistake. This was an enormous amount of money in the early days of IBM. Tom Watson, the founder and CEO, summoned the dejected junior executive to his office. Thinking that he was about to be fired, the young executive laid his letter of resignation on Mr. Watson's desk, "I guess you've called me in for my resignation. Here it is. I resign."

Watson replied, "You must be joking. I just invested ten million dollars educating you. I can't afford to accept your resignation."

This remarkable act of forgiveness empowered the junior executive who went on to become instrumental in building the corporate giant, IBM. You see, forgiveness is a form of empowerment. Empowering others is what leadership is all about. Effective leaders cultivate a culture of forgiveness that enables people to strengthen their abilities, grow, take risks, and lead others through the maze of colossal change and challenge. When you stop to think about it, that's exactly what God has done for you. Then, God commands that you also forgive others. Effective leaders work hard at cultivating this important leadership attribute. Leaders read, attend seminars, implement what they have learned, experiment, fail, and try again in their untiring efforts to establish and build a culture of forgiveness.

The relational model of leadership is a perspective that is sorely missing in most popular notions about leadership. In fact, many leadership models warn against building relationships—arguing that productivity will always suffer when relationships are established with co-workers and subordinates. Consequently, twenty-first century organizations are marked by loneliness and isolation. Individual isolation is, unfortunately, one of the odd characteristics of our culture today. There is less and less interpersonal interaction at home, work, church, school, and neighborhoods. Technology is replacing social intimacy. More and more people are living alone, working alone, studying alone, and "bowling alone." There is a significant loss of social capital causing fear, distrust, and insecurity, which leads to loss of effectiveness and productivity. Restoring this relational model of leadership to your cultural institutions is a strategic response to the isolation and bitter loneliness of those who find themselves "lost" in the midst of urban society. It is your key to effective leadership.

## Cultivating Relational Leadership

As in previous chapters, I encourage you to initiate two simple action steps that will enable you to cultivate this important leadership trait. First, complete the "Personal Reflection" exercise at the end of this chapter. Take time to thoughtfully and intentionally reflect on each question before recording your responses. Continue to invest quality time in responding to each question.

Second, complete the "Cultivating Your Created Leadership Capacity" exercise, also found at the end of this chapter. This exercise will help you think through how best to apply relational leadership in each one of your major life roles and spheres of influence. Remember, like God, you possess the capacity for intentional and interpersonal relationships, emphasizing high regard for the well-being and personhood of others.

You are relational. You are a leader. This is the truth about leadership! This is the *Genesis Principle of Leadership*.

# Personal Reflection

### *Leaders Are Relational*

- Leadership is reclaiming and cultivating your God-given, created attributes. What specific action steps will you take to develop this leadership trait: Relational?

- What does it mean that God is relational?

- List three ways in which God has been relational to you:

- List some specific actions you can take to be relational to others:

- Which action will you implement this week?

- To whom?

- What result(s) do you expect from taking this action?

- Take a few moments—now—to pray about this action.

- In what way(s) could you help someone in your family, workplace, or community to claim and cultivate this leadership attribute in his life?

- Cultivate this created leadership trait by completing the "Cultivating Your Created Leadership Capacity" exercise on the next page.

## Cultivating Your Created Leadership Capacity

Leadership is the lifelong pursuit of claiming and cultivating your God-created attributes.

1. Select a Life Role (e.g. Leader, Spouse, Parent, Worker, Neighbor, etc.).

2. List the key Duties and Responsibilities of that Life Role.

3. Then design and list specific Action Steps that will enable you to steward this leadership attribute.

## Cultivating Relational Leadership

As a leader you are capable of developing intentional and interpersonal relationships, emphasizing high regard for the well-being and personhood of others.

## LIFE ROLE:

_____

Duties/Responsibilities:     Leadership is Action:

1. _____ | _____
   _____ | _____

2. _____ | _____
   _____ | _____

3. _____ | _____
   _____ | _____

4. _____ | _____
   _____ | _____

5. _____ | _____
   _____ | _____

6. _____ | _____
   _____ | _____

7. _____ | _____
   _____ | _____

*What you do with what you know is what*
*Christian knowing is all about.* (Os Guinness)

# Leaders are Free and Responsible

As a leader you possess the ability to independently make meaningful choices, the freedom to act upon your choices, and the personal responsibility for the consequences of your decisions and actions.

## Run! Run as Fast as You Can!

It was an ear-splitting, thunderous crack—the kind that every boy dreams of, that makes heroes, that serves as fodder for blockbuster movies—the kind of hit that Babe Ruth, Ted Williams, and the legendary Bull Durham could only fantasize about.

The ball seemed suspended in time and space as it floated ever so slowly and softly over home plate. My wooden, "Fred Lynn" autographed, Louisville Slugger was eagerly poised over my right shoulder, cocked and loaded for destruction. The lettering on the softball was so vivid, "Rawlings Official Softball." I could actually see each individual thread of its bright red stitching.

The pitch was so "juicy" as it floated into the strike zone. I swung my treasured "Fred Lynn" with all the might a sixth-grader could muster. Oh, how I nailed that ball - so hard - so squarely! I saw the ball actually flatten to half its diameter against the Louisville Slugger. The red-stitched Rawlings exploded off my bat, launched like a rocket into the cloudless, deep blue sky. Higher and higher and farther and farther it soared. I slowly let the bat slip into the tips of my fingers, partially dragging it in the dirt as I started my victory lap around the bases. I didn't really run. I walked, mostly, slowly, dramatically, triumphantly, taking great care not to lose sight of this white missile. I savored this mind-blowing moment as the ball soared farther and farther and farther. "Back—back—back." I could hear, faintly, the exuberant cheers of my classmates as the leather-covered Rawlings rocketed into the universe.

This magical moment, my "15 seconds of fame," ended abruptly with the shattering sound of exploding glass. The Rawlings, launched by my legendary, epic-making blast, crashed through the large, plate glass window into the sixth-grade classroom on the second floor of Lincoln Elementary School. The cheers of the "roaring crowd" suddenly turned into hissing gasps of horror and disbelief. Instantly, my schoolmates disappeared. In the proverbial "twinkling of an eye," they were gone! I was frozen with disbelief! I couldn't believe my eyes—or ears. The large, expensive, triple-paned, plate glass window was destroyed. There I was, standing alone near second base, in a state of supreme shock; my "Fred Lynn" autographed "Louisville Slugger" hanging limply in my right hand.

The silence was numbing, deafening—except for the ear-piercing, siren-like shrieks of Ms. Gertrude Trumble, my teacher. Ms. Trumble seemed to materialize out of thin air just as fast as the Rawlings and my classmates had disappeared. She didn't run. She didn't really walk. She waddled, slowly, determined, stalking me with laser precision. She was fully armed with her dreaded paddle, her own version of the "Louisville Slugger," autographed with the signatures of her previous "victims." With each deliberate step she slapped her right thigh with her instrument of doom. My fate was certain as she stormed closer—ever closer—step by deliberate step.

Terror gripped my life! I looked for the nearest path of escape. I was desperate to find the quickest way to flee from this "fire-breathing dragon," lumbering in my direction. Frantically, I looked left, snapped my head back to the right, and quickly glanced over both shoulders. No matter where I looked, all I could see was the twelve foot high chain link fence that surrounded the playground—blocking every possibility of escape. Ms. Trumble, huffing and puffing and bellowing and tramping my way, was the one terrifying obstacle to emancipation from the horror that was about to launch *me* into outer space.

What was I to do? I was frozen with fear. I had been on the receiving end of Ms. Trumble's "Louisville Slugger" before. My own autograph was indelibly etched into her paddle—more than once. And my Father's words echoed through my mind, "You get a whippin' at school—you'll get another whippin' when you get home!"

Still there was this compelling voice, "Run! Run as fast as you can!" Yet I heard another of my Father's admonitions, "When you do something wrong, you fess up. Take your punishment like a man!" Oh, how I wanted to evaporate, to escape my pending doom, now just paces away, and forget that all this had happened! Where were my "faithful" friends? I was in a tight spot. And it was about to get tighter. And there I stood, alone, face to face with my "executioner." There was no escape. My doom was sure! I had to take my punishment—like a man, right there on the playground, in the middle of what just a few seconds ago was my "field of dreams."

Not only did I suffer the "wrath" of Ms. Trumble for breaking the schoolhouse window, I received the promised punishment from my father's razor strap that evening. Then, to add further pain and humiliation, I had to stay after school for a month, washing windows, to work off the replacement cost of the window I broke with my "made-for-television," epic-making homerun. I was the talk of the school for weeks—not because of this history-making blast during recess, but because I was paddled by Ms. Trumble—before God and a watching world. I didn't like it. It was painful—in more ways than one. With my father's admonition and the "smack" of the paddle ringing in my ears, I took full responsibility for breaking the schoolhouse window.

## In a Tight Spot?

What are you to do when you are in a "tight spot"? Every day, in every arena of your life, you are faced with making choices. Fortunately, most choices are small and seem to be unimportant: "What color of socks shall I wear today?" "What shall I order for lunch?" "What movie shall I watch tonight?" From time to time, you face much larger, more challenging decisions: "Whom shall I marry?" "Should I treat my cancer with chemo or radiation? Or shall I treat it at all?" "Do I really want to abide by my dying spouse's living will?" Life is filled with making choices and coping with the consequences of those choices. Indeed, every choice entails assuming the responsibility for how that choice impacts your own life and the lives of those around you.

Your ability to make decisions comes from God. The Creator equipped you with the freedom to make choices (both small and large) and has granted you full responsibility for those choices. In fact, God expects you to make decisions. He also expects you to be fully responsible for the consequences of your decisions. However, the "conventional wisdom" of the day would have you believe that people are helpless victims incapable of making decisions for themselves. The modern view of personhood would have you believe that you are the product of and are helplessly bound to the fatalistic environmental chains of familial circumstances, the random roll of the genetic dice, the press of the culture, uncontrollable socioeconomic factors, or, if there is a God, the pre-determination of a merciless, uncaring deity. Simply stated, you are but a "victim" of your genetics and/or your environment. Therefore, you expect one of two things. You either expect someone else (parents, teachers, governmental agencies, physicians, health insurance companies, or others) to make decisions for you, or you expect someone else to take responsibility for your decisions since, it was someone else's fault for your choice anyway.

## The Biblical Perspective on Decision Making

The biblical view is quite different. The Bible teaches that you were created in the image of God. You possess most of God's attributes. God not only gave you the ability to make your own choices, but He also gave you the freedom and responsibility to make choices, small and large. I like the way the Catholic Church described this important biblical truth in *The Catechism of the Catholic Church*. According to this document, God gave you "...the capacity to act or not to act, to do this or that, and so to perform deliberate actions on one's own responsibility."[51] Or as Rabbi Shimon Apisdorf expressed it, you have "...the capacity to express in one's life those values and ideals which stem from the essence of the human soul." In other words, as bearers of the image of God, you possess the ability to see yourself, and others, as Rabbi Apisdorf further explains, "...as shapers, creators, and captains of great ships of potential."[52]

As a free moral agent you possess the created freedom and ability to independently make meaningful choices. You possess the freedom to act or not act out your choices. Therefore, you are responsible for your actions. When you choose, you must also accept the consequences of your choices (both positive and negative) on your life and the lives of others impacted by your choices. There was a sense in which my decision to swing that bat was also a choice to risk breaking that window and accept the "stinging" consequences of Ms. Trumble's punishment.

## Mindless Robots?

You are not destined to live reflexively, mindlessly reacting to relentless genetic and environmental stimuli bombarding you. God has given you the freedom to make choices. You are a free moral agent. In other words, you possess the freedom to choose. You possess the independent freedom to act upon, or not to act upon, your impulses. Although every fiber of your being conspires to force a particular decision upon you, God has granted you the freedom to choose otherwise. Faced with a choice between good and evil, you are free to choose either. This freedom, this capacity, is much more that a trivial liberty that some benevolent deity has bestowed upon you. It is both an expectation and a power. You are expected to reclaim and cultivate this attribute. Your use of this attribute is not to be taken lightly. In the final analysis, you are responsible for the proper use of your God-given capacity to choose and take responsibility for your decisions.

From time to time there will be certain circumstances where you will be forced to choose between an obvious good and an obvious evil (e.g. "Do I kick that puppy or do I scratch him behind the ears?"). In such cases, God demands your obedience to His revealed will. He expects you to obey and follow His explicit instructions written to us in the Bible. Though God is completely in control of every aspect of the universe, He does not coerce us. He made us free and responsible. He expects you to choose the path prescribed in His Law. In each example, the implicit assumption is that you are free to follow or not to follow. For instance, in the Old Testament Book of Leviticus, God instructs you to be holy. He says, "For I am the LORD who brought you up out of the land of Egypt to be your God. You shall therefore be holy, for I am holy" (Leviticus 11:45, ESV). Similarly, in Deuteronomy Moses instructs, "You shall be careful therefore to do as the Lord your God has commanded you. You shall not turn aside to the right hand or to the left" (Deuteronomy 5:32, ESV). These are explicit commands. God expects you to obey.

There is another excellent example in Numbers. In this passage, God's people are traveling through the wilderness; God was out in front leading the way: "Then the angel of the Lord went ahead and stood in a narrow place, where there was no way to turn either to the right or to the left" (Numbers 22:26, ESV). In such instances God desires that you choose the prescribed path. You are to follow Him in holiness—obediently. This requires that you know all of His commands—His moral will. If you are to obey God's commands, you must know what these commands are. Obedience, then, begins with reading God's Word, The Holy Bible, written for you and me. The more you know His Word, the more your choices will obediently reflect His commands and desires for you.

Yet, there are other circumstances in which you will be forced to choose between two relative goods. For example, do I take the job in Cincinnati or the job in Indianapolis? Do I enroll my children in a public school or in a private school? In such cases, there is a sense in which God expects you to take leadership when making these choices. I am utterly fascinated with a remarkable picture in Isaiah: "Whether you turn to the right or to the left, your ears will hear a voice behind you, saying, 'This is the way; walk in it'" (Isaiah 30:21, NIV). Many times throughout the Holy Scriptures, you see God standing out front, leading, directing, and showing the way. But in this instance, God is not out front, showing the way. You are out front; God is following behind you. What an amazing picture! You are out front. God is "behind" you. When you come to a turn in the road, God says, "You decide! Turn to the right or turn to the left. I am behind you. You lead. You decide. I am behind you. I will bless you. And you will hear me say, This is the way. Walk thee in it."

Too many people are crippled by indecision, irrationality, and unwarranted emotionally-laden judgments. Too many people experience unnecessary paralysis in their attempt to find God's "perfect" will in every detail of their lives—even down to trying to decide which specific salad dressing God "wants" them to eat on their luncheon salad. The reality that God grants the freedom to choose can be a bit unnerving for those with an earnest desire to know God's pinpoint, perfect will in every detail of life. The point is this: God's "perfect will" is for you to make your own choice in most situations.

In his best-selling book, *Decision Making and the Will of God*, Garry Friesen pointed out that when you ask, "How can I know the will of God?" you are asking the "wrong" question. Instead, Friesen argued that a better question to ask is, "How do I make good decisions?"[53] When I first read this statement, I jumped up and yelled, "Yes!" As a free and responsible creature, you need to be better equipped, taught as it were, to make free and responsible decisions. When faced with the decision between an obvious evil and an obvious good, you need to be equipped to follow the path prescribed by God's Word. When faced with a choice between two relative goods, you need the assurance and confidence of knowing that God is backing you up. In the pursuit of a decision, I suggest attending a decision-making seminar, reading a good book like Dr. Friesen's classic book on decision making, or adopting and using a good decision-making model. Such things will be invaluable as you cultivate this long-lost freedom and responsibility.

## Free to Lead

Effective leaders exercise their freedom to choose to act or not to act. Effective leaders take full responsibility for the consequences of their choices, good or bad, on their life and the lives of others. Effective leaders are accountable for how this created attribute, free and responsible, has been carried out. Yes, there is a price, both immediate and future, for the exercise of this great gift of free and responsible leadership. As free moral agents, leaders know they are responsible, that is accountable for every one of their actions—small and large. In other words, leaders must choose wisely and act responsibly. If you hit a softball through the school house window, you are responsible and are to be held accountable for the broken window. If you murder another person, you are answerable to the civil government for that death. If you commit a sin toward God, you are held responsible and accountable to God for that sin. In every choice and action in your life, you're answerable for your choices, actions, and obligations.

There is both an immediate and future dimension to this responsibility. In the present tense, you will suffer reward or loss from others for your actions. In the future tense, you will suffer reward or loss when you give a full account of your choices and actions to God. You will, one day, stand before the Creator and give Him a full accounting for every word, action, and deed, or lack thereof. "If the work that anyone has built on the foundation survives, he will receive reward. If anyone's work is burned up, he will suffer loss, though he himself will be saved, but only as through fire" (I Corinthians 3:14–15, ESV).

## Cultivating Free and Responsible Leadership

There are two simple action steps that will enable you to cultivate this important leadership trait. First, complete the "Personal Reflection" exercise at the end of this chapter. Take time to thoughtfully and intentionally reflect on each question before recording your responses. Continue to invest quality time in responding to each question.

Second, complete the "Cultivating Your Created Leadership Capacity" exercise, also found at the end of this chapter. This exercise will help you think through how best to apply free and responsible leadership in each one of your major life roles and spheres of influence. Remember, like God, you possess the ability to independently make meaningful choices, the freedom to act or not act out your choices, and the personal responsibility for the consequences of your decisions and actions.

You are free and responsible. You are a leader. This is the truth about leadership! This is the *Genesis Principle of Leadership*.

# Personal Reflection

## *Leaders Are Free and Responsible*

- Leadership is reclaiming and cultivating your God-given, created attributes. What specific action steps will you take to develop this leadership trait: Free and Responsible?

- What does it mean that God is free and responsible?

- List three ways in which God has been free and responsible to you:

- List some specific actions you can take to be free and responsible to others:

- Which action will you implement this week?

- To whom?

- What result(s) do you expect from taking this action?

- Take a few moments—now—to pray about this action.

- In what way(s) could you help someone in your family, workplace, or community to claim and cultivate this leadership attribute in his life?

- Cultivate this created leadership trait by completing the "Cultivating Your Created Leadership Capacity" exercise on the next page.

## Cultivating Your Created Leadership Capacity

Leadership is the lifelong pursuit of claiming and cultivating your God-created attributes.

1. Select a Life Role (e.g. Leader, Spouse, Parent, Worker, Neighbor, etc.).

2. List the key Duties and Responsibilities of that Life Role.

3. Then design and list specific Action Steps that will enable you to steward this leadership attribute.

## Cultivating Free and Responsible Leadership

As a leader you possess the ability to independently make meaningful choices, the freedom to act upon your choices, and the personal responsibility for the consequences of your decisions and actions.

## Life Role:

_____

| Duties/Responsibilities: | Leadership is Action: |
|---|---|
| 1. | |
| 2. | |
| 3. | |
| 4. | |
| 5. | |
| 6. | |
| 7. | |

*What you do with what you know is what Christian knowing is all about.* (Os Guinness)

# Leaders Are Loving

As a leader you possess the ability to love and be loved. By divine nature, calling, and duty, you are to love God and others at all times by doing what is best for them and practicing forgiveness.

## Love 'Em and Lead 'Em

Recipient of the Distinguished Flying Cross and the Bronze Star, the highly decorated Major General John Henry Stanford served in several key command assignments during his thirty-one years of illustrious service in the United States Army. This service to his country included heroic tours of duty in Korea, Vietnam, and Desert Shield/Desert Storm. Following his retirement from active military service in 1991, Stanford was elected to county manager of Fulton County, Georgia (a county that holds Atlanta within its boundaries). Though he served for just four years, he was heralded for his visionary and progressive approach to public service. He was described by many as a "local hero making a difference."

In 1995, Stanford took on a bigger challenge, superintendent of the "troubled" Seattle public school system. Again, his visionary, progressive, "can-do" style of leadership earned him national acclaim—including an invitation to address the delegates of the 1996 Democratic National Convention. Tragically, Stanford's tenure as superintendent of the Seattle public schools was cut short by his premature death from leukemia in 1998. But in an amazingly short period of time he identified and aggressively attacked several serious problems, including dismal academic achievement, school violence, low morale, and inadequate funding. It didn't take him long to earn the respect and admiration of everyone who knew and worked with him.

Stanford had a charismatic personality, infectious grin, a twinkle in his eye, a wry sense of humor, and unbridled energy and enthusiasm. He never stopped being a kid and was often seen riding his unicycle in school rallies and hallways. He believed in, and held to, a leadership philosophy he called "Love 'em and Lead 'em." By this he meant that, "You must love people with all that the term love connotes—even though some will not love you back—because it's the best tool you have." He added, "I have found that if you love people, you will get more than you ever imagined." On another occasion Stanford commented,

> Everyone has the potential to be a great leader. Someone once said, "There are at least four things you can do with your hands. You can wring them in despair; you can fold them in idleness; you can clench them in anger; or you can use them to help others." If you want to be a great leader please remember to use not only your hands but also your heart and remember to Love 'em and Lead 'em.

And "love 'em" he did. As one school board member remembered, "John Stanford is my hero because he taught me that in each of us is someone who can make a difference. He believed that in each of us is someone who can love the world and who is passionate and unendingly optimistic."[54] His loving leadership made a profound impact on the students as well. One student recalled, "He (John Stanford) brought a warm, safe, and embracing feeling to the normally lonely feeling in the school."[55]

## Loving Leadership?

By now you may be thinking, "Loving leadership? Love your employees in the twenty-first century? What a ridiculous idea!" "Tough times call for tough leaders—emotionless, cold, calculating, commandeering, aggressive, cigar-chomping, fire-breathing dragons!" "This is a new day—a new age—there's no room for this touchy-feely-loving stuff!" "Loving leadership? Why, we'll go under!" "You don't realize what it takes to be a leader these days!" Browse through the business section of your favorite bookstore and you will find similar sentiments reflected in many of the books on leadership. Such books claim to house the one irreplaceable factor or formula for leading successfully. And astonishingly many end up promoting this sort of take-charge, aggressive, emotionless style of leadership.

Does the name "Chainsaw Al Dunlap" ring a bell for you? Al Dunlap, the notorious turnaround guru of the corporate world, is the undisputed poster boy for the stereotypical corporate leader of the twenty-first century. Dunlap, the self-proclaimed "stockholder's friend" and "Rambo in pinstripes," became the darling of corporate America for his uncanny ability to turn around financially troubled corporations. Stockholders loved Dunlap for his ability to inflate corporate earnings and the value of their stockholdings. But as time went along, investors learned the stark truth about Chainsaw Al Dunlap. Dunlap's uncanny ability at turning around troubled companies was a deception of smoke and mirrors. In the wake of his slash-and-burn tactics lay the horrific reality of professional and financial lives ruined as he destroyed companies for personal financial gain. One person described Dunlap's strategy as something "akin to burning the walls to heat the house." Bruce Fenton, in his article for the "Fenton Report," an online wealth management newsletter, called Dunlap a "pro at window dressing troubled corporations."[56] In the final analysis, Chainsaw Al Dunlap represents a spectacular, eye-opening portrayal of the worst kind of leadership. Dunlap epitomized the take-charge, aggressive, emotionless, win-at-all-costs style of leadership.

Yes—courageous, focused, determined, and hard-working leaders are needed in twenty-first century organizations. Dozens of organizations collapse every day for the lack of effective leaders. But as Christopher Loving, Founder and President of LIFT (Loving Institute for Tomorrow), observed in his on-line audio book,

> We can no longer afford to graduate bright, talented, and competent lawyers, architects, and marketing executives. Today, the world needs leaders who not only have great minds, but great hearts as well. [57]

Actually, loving leadership is an ancient paradigm—a very old prescription for effective leadership. It may surprise you to learn that loving leadership is actually a biblical model. In fact, it is God's model, and it is just as effective in the twenty-first century as when God first came up with the idea. God created you to love and to be loved. It is your divine calling and duty to love God and others at all times. You are to regard others more highly than you regard yourself, do what is best for them, and practice forgiveness. There are three essential leadership qualities of loving leadership found in this definition. First, God is the supreme example of love. Second, you are to love God. Third, you are to love others.

First, loving leadership requires recognizing God as the supreme model of love. During an interview, a reporter asked Karl Barth, the famous theologian, what was his most remarkable theological discovery. After a few moments of reflection Barth responded, "Jesus loves me this I know, for the Bible tells me so." Karl Barth, unlike few other people, had explored the depths and riches of the knowledge of God. After all was said and done, Barth understood a simple truth, God is love. Children of all ages have proclaimed in song and in good works this simple, but profound, reality, God is the emphasis and perfection of love. Indeed, it is a truth revealed to mankind throughout the Bible:

> Anyone who does not love does not know God, because God is love.
>
> I John 4:8 (ESV)

> But God shows his love for us in that while we were still sinners, Christ died for us.
>
> Romans 5:8 (ESV)

> For God so loved the world, that he gave his only Son, that whoever believes in him should not perish but have eternal life.
>
> John 3:16 (ESV)

Yes, learn all you can about God. But in the final analysis, know that God is love. For it is God's amazing, eternal, and unconditional love that is at the center of all His mighty, all-encompassing acts of grace—creation, redemption, and consummation. It is also the motivation for His tender and gracious interactions with you. God is love; God is the fountain of love; and, God created you to love and be loved.

Second, leaders are to love God. You are to be obedient to God's first and great command: "And he said to them, 'You shall love the Lord your God with all your heart and with all your soul and with all your mind. This is the great and first commandment'" (Matthew 22:37–38, ESV). Every beat of your heart, the inner-most depths of your soul, and every microscopic neuron of your mind is to focus, pursue, and engage this loving God. Love God with every fiber of your being. Why? Because God loves you. He did not have to love—there is nothing in Him that needs your love. Yet in His sovereign grace, God always treats you better than you deserve. Therefore, the Bible teaches you to love God, because He first loved (1 John 4:19, ESV). When you know and experience the breadth and length and height and depth of that love (Ephesians 3:18, ESV) your cold heart cannot help but be warmed and melted. You cannot help but love Him passionately in return. As the famous Puritan preacher Thomas Watson observed, "If ice melts, it is because the sun has shone upon it; so if the frozen heart melts in love, it is because the Sun of Righteousness has shone upon it."[58]

Third, leaders are called to love others with the same degree of passion and potency that God has loved them. After stating that your obligation to respond to God's love is with love for God, Jesus adds, "And the second is like it: You shall love your neighbor as yourself" (Matthew 22:39, ESV). Knowing and experiencing God's love carries with it certain obligations—obligations that are summarized by Jesus himself. Imagine—the whole of the Bible boils down to these two points—love God and love others.

Effective leaders not only know personally and intimately

God's love, effective leaders practice the love they know and have received. Leaders love others at all times—every time, every day, every night. Leaders allow Christ to be the example of how to love others:

> So if there is any encouragement in Christ, any comfort from love, any participation in the Spirit, any affection and sympathy, complete my joy by being of the same mind, having the same love, being in full accord and of one mind. Do nothing from rivalry or conceit, but in humility count others more significant than yourselves. Let each of you look not only to his own interests, but also to the interests of others. Have this mind among yourselves, which is yours in Christ Jesus, who, though he was in the form of God, did not count equality with God a thing to be grasped, but made himself nothing, taking the form of a servant, being born in the likeness of men. And being found in human form, he humbled himself by becoming obedient to the point of death, even death on a cross.
>
> Philippians 2:1–8 (ESV)

Leaders love at all times. Loving leadership is not a "tool" that you take out of your leadership tool kit from time to time and then return casually as if love is a cosmic game of "good cop—bad cop." Because love is part and parcel of your created nature, love is a permanent component of your leadership arsenal and is to be employed at all times. Love is at the epicenter of everything you do in every arena of your life—no matter what you endeavor to accomplish. Whether you are fetching a cup of coffee, moving mountains, resurrecting a dead company, or offering yourself up to be burned at the stake, love is the central, driving force for effective leadership. In the final analysis, you can accomplish nothing; you are nothing; and, you gain nothing outside the context of love. The Apostle Paul spoke about this way of love to the Christians in Corinth:

> If I speak in the tongues of men and of angels, but have not love, I am a noisy gong or a clanging cymbal. And if I have prophetic powers, and understand all mysteries and all knowledge, and if I have all faith, so as to remove mountains, but have not love, I am nothing. If I give away all I have, and if I deliver up my body to be burned, but have not love, I gain nothing.
>
> I Corinthians 13:1–3 (ESV)

You may have a brilliant, highly educated, and disciplined mind; you may possess matchless leadership experience and success; and, you may possess unparalleled faith and hope. God says, "…the greatest of these is love" (I Corinthians 13:13, ESV). A day is coming when all your leadership traits and accomplishments will fail you—even pass away. But this attribute, love, will remain. Faith, hope and love may be the bedrock of life now, but there will be a day when even faith and hope will no longer be needed. In that day, love will literally be all that is necessary.

Love has multiple meanings in today's culture. I "love" ice cream. I "love" my dog. I "love" you. Let's make "love." These mixed, and often selfish, definitions can't help but distort and confuse this notion of loving leadership. But God does not leave you to second guess the qualitative dimension of love. As you continue to read the apostle's "love chapter," (I Corinthians 13), you will observe that love is patient, kind, not envious, not boastful, not proud, not rude, not self-seeking, not easily angered, keeps no record of wrongs, does not delight in evil, rejoices in the truth, protects, trusts, hopes, perseveres, and never fails. Loving leadership, cultivated and stewarded around these qualities, is effective leadership—at all times.

Leaders regard others more highly than they regard themselves. I call this the "Philippian Principle of Leadership." "Do nothing from rivalry or conceit, but in humility count others more significant than yourself" (Philippians 2:3, ESV). A lot is said these days about the concept of "servant-leadership." Sometimes the discussion of servant-leadership can grow complex and confusing. Nevertheless, there is one principle that must emerge in any biblical definition of servant-leadership: effective leaders must love in the same way Christ loves those He leads. Loving leaders do not expect their subordinates to make them look good; loving leaders always regard their subordinates more highly, more significantly, than they regard themselves. Following the example of Jesus, loving leaders humble themselves, make themselves nothing, and take on the form of a servant—elevating those around them—looking to the interests of others. Loving leaders are determined to do what it takes to make their subordinates look good.

> Let each of you look not only to his own interests, but also to the interests of others. Have this mind among yourselves, which is yours in Christ Jesus, who, though he was in the form of God, did not count equality with God a thing to be grasped, but made himself nothing, taking the form of a servant, being born in the likeness of men. And being found in human form, he humbled himself by becoming obedient to the point of death, even death on a cross.
>
> Philippians 2:4–8 (ESV)

Leaders do what is best for others. Often this can be a difficult challenge when a leader is forced to make a choice between what others "want" and what is "best." Too often, because of a desperate need to be loved, you might be tempted to acquiesce to another person's wants, in the vain hope that they will "love" you. Or, perhaps, you actually fear that they will not love you in return. Later, unfortunately, you will discover, the hard way, that caving in did not produce the kind of results you were hoping for. Doing what is best is a challenging task. Perhaps, the best guideline—or rule of thumb—is Jesus' words: "So whatever you wish that others would do to you, do also to them, for this is the law and the prophets" (Matthew 7:12, ESV).

What is known as the "Golden Rule," also called the "Ethic of Reciprocity," has become a universal ethical principle found in many religions and philosophies around the globe. There are multiple versions appearing in practically every religious group and culture, including Egyptian religions, Confucianism, Baha'i, Islam, and others. Doing what is best for others is a crucial characteristic of effective leaders understood by peoples throughout the ages.

Regarding others more highly than you regard yourself is the key to reconciliation. People do not always see eye to eye on every issue—perhaps most issues. Therefore, reconciliation is a vitally necessary ingredient in effective leadership. Differences of opinion that are not managed well can lead to distorted, destructive, and sinful behaviors. In such circumstances, loving leaders take the lead in repairing these broken, distorted, and disappointing relationships by initiating and practicing reconciliation. I find it interesting that God provided a biblical recipe that serves as a guideline for reconciliation. Several, seemingly impossible, differences have been resolved following the biblical principles found in Matthew 18. Indeed, there is not a more compelling summary of biblical reconciliation than the words of Jesus recorded in this passage of Scripture:

> If your brother sins against you go and tell him his fault, between you and him alone. If he listens to you, you have gained your brother. But if he does not listen, take one or two others along with you, that every charge may be established by the evidence of two or three witnesses. If he refuses to listen to them, tell it to the church. And if he refuses to listen even to the church, let him be to you as a Gentile and a tax collector. Truly, I say to you, whatever you bind on earth shall be bound in heaven, and whatever you loose on earth shall be loosed in heaven. Again I say to you, if two of you agree on earth about anything they ask, it will be done for them by my Father in heaven. For where two or three are gathered in my name, there am I among them." Then Peter came up and said to him, "Lord, how often will my brother sin against me, and I forgive him? As many as seven times?" Jesus said to him, "I do not say to you seven times, but seventy times seven.
>
> Matthew 18:15–22 (ESV)

Remember, conflict that arises from differences of opinion is not an incidental or unnecessary speed bump on the road of life. Conflict is not something you must, at all costs, get behind you so that you can get on with life. Conflict *is* life! As such it must be handled with great skill and care. God's Word, the Bible, provides you with a simple, ancient, time-tested, powerful, and effective recipe for dealing with differences of opinion. Yes—these timeless principles are remarkably different from the emotional, combative, often litigious ways by which many people cope with differences these days. But when these principles are applied, they provide a courageous and effective opportunity to glorify God, to serve others, to grow in Christ-likeness, and to become an effective leader.

Loving is a remarkable leadership attribute. Effective leaders love people enough not to allow hostility or differences of opinion to damage, distort, or destroy an otherwise productive relationship. In fact, reconciliation is an important dimension of love. The Apostle Paul said as much in Ephesians 2:13–16 (ESV):

> But now in Christ Jesus you who once were far off have been brought near by the blood of Christ. For he himself is our peace, who has made us both one and has broken down in his flesh the dividing wall of hostility by abolishing the law of commandments and ordinances, that he might create in himself one new man in place of the two, so making peace, and might reconcile us both to God in one body through the cross, thereby killing the hostility.

God loves you. God reconciled you to Himself, through Christ, so that you might experience reconciliation between each other. Effective leaders pursue reconciliation with others because God pursued reconciliation with them.

## Cultivating Loving Leadership

Reclaim, cultivate, and steward this leadership attribute, loving, in every arena of your life: home, workplace, neighborhood, community, and church. Again, allow me to encourage you to pursue two simple actions that will enable you to cultivate this important leadership trait. First, complete the "Personal Reflection" exercise at the end of this chapter. Take time to thoughtfully and intentionally reflect on each question before recording your responses. Continue to invest quality time in responding to each question.

Second, complete the "Cultivating Your Created Leadership Capacity" exercise, also found at the end of this chapter. This exercise will help you think through how best to apply loving leadership in each one of your major life roles and spheres of influence. Remember, like God, you possess the ability to love and to be loved. By divine nature, calling, and duty you are to love God and others at all times doings what is best for them and by practicing forgiveness and reconciliation.

You are loving. You are a leader. This is the truth about leadership! This is the *Genesis Principle of Leadership*.

# Personal Reflection

### *Leaders Are Loving*

- Leadership is reclaiming and cultivating your God-given, created attributes. What specific action steps will you take to develop this leadership trait: Loving?

- What does it mean that God is loving?

- List three ways in which God has been loving to you:

- List some specific actions you can take to be loving to others:

- Which action will you implement this week?

- To whom?

- What result(s) do you expect from taking this action?

- Take a few moments—now—to pray about this action.

- In what way(s) could you help someone in your family, workplace, or community to claim and cultivate this leadership attribute in his life?

- Cultivate this created leadership trait by completing the "Cultivating Your Created Leadership Capacity" exercise on the next page.

## Cultivating Your Created Leadership Capacity

Leadership is the lifelong pursuit of claiming and cultivating your God-created attributes.

1. Select a Life Role (e.g. Leader, Spouse, Parent, Worker, Neighbor, etc.).
2. List the key Duties and Responsibilities of that Life Role.
3. Then design and list specific Action Steps that will enable you to steward this leadership attribute.

## Cultivating Loving Leadership

As a leader you possess the ability to love and be loved. By divine nature, calling, and duty, you are to love God and others at all times by doing what is best for them and practicing forgiveness.

# LIFE ROLE:

_____

Duties/Responsibilities:     Leadership is Action:

1. _____

2. _____

3. _____

4. _____

5. _____

6. _____

7. _____

*What you do with what you know is what Christian knowing is all about.* (Os Guinness)

# Leaders are Merciful

As a leader you are called upon to be actively gracious and compassionate toward the well-being and peace of others through acts of favor and mercy—even to those who do not desire or deserve it.

## "He Was Hungry, So I Cooked Him Breakfast."

How is it that a young, single mom, bound by fear and terrified by the knowledge of the murderous deeds of her captor, could calmly prepare a breakfast of eggs and pancakes, engage her assailant in meaningful and purposeful conversation, encourage him to surrender to the authorities, and give a desperate fugitive hope, meaning, and purpose in the darkest hour of his life? How can we ever forget Ashley Smith's story of undeserved mercy? Her story is now a part of American folklore told in books, television specials, and movies.

March 12, 2005—Duluth, Georgia—2:30 a.m. Ashley Smith suddenly found herself held at gunpoint at the entrance to her new apartment. "Do you know who I am?" the assailant asked.

Not until he removed his hat did Ashley realize that her captor was the subject of the largest manhunt in Georgia history. Just a few hours earlier, prisoner Brian Nichols overpowered a deputy in an Atlanta courthouse, gunned down the judge and a court reporter, shot and killed yet another deputy as he fled the courthouse, and later killed a federal agent taking the agent's truck in his desperate attempt to flee the law.

Now Ashley was being held hostage by this desperado. Her hands and feet were bound with masking tape and electrical cords. Though terrified and fearful for her life, Ashley engaged Nichols in conversation, telling him about her little five-year-old daughter, her difficult life, and how her husband had been killed in a stabbing just a few years earlier. Soon, Nichols untied her hands and feet and allowed Ashley to go to her bedroom to get some things to read. She returned with a book called, *The Purpose Driven Life: What on Earth Am I Here For?* and began to read aloud from Chapter 33: "How Real Servants Act." Nichols was captivated by the first paragraph of this chapter. "Stop! Read that part again!" The two were soon engaged in a deep and meaningful conversation about the meaning and purpose of life. Nichol's demeanor toward Ashley softened. He called her "his sister in Christ" and an "angel sent from God."

Ashley fixed a breakfast of eggs and pancakes for Nichols, later explaining, "He was hungry, so I cooked him breakfast." They talked about God, family, miracles, purpose, and hope. Ashley encouraged Nichols to turn himself in to the police. As Ashley put it later, "And he really, honestly, when I looked at him, he looked like he didn't want to do it anymore."

Miraculously, around 9:30 a.m., knowing that Ashley would turn him in, Nichols allowed her to leave to "pick up her daughter from church." Ashley immediately called 9–1-1. Within moments, the apartment complex was surrounded by law enforcement officials. Nichols waved a white flag and surrendered, without incident, to the S.W.A.T. team. Ashley watched from behind a parked van. Ashley believes there was a purpose for being abducted by Nichols, "I believe God brought him to my door so he couldn't hurt anyone else."

## Uncommon?

Ashley's story of uncommon mercy is not as rare and unusual as you might think. The Bible is filled with wonderful accounts of people being concerned for the well-being of others, even if the other person did not deserve it. Jesus' parable of the Good Samaritan is one of the most famous and widely known stories in the New Testament. Jesus tells the story about a man who had been beaten and robbed and left to die by the side of the road. Strangely, everyone, including a priest and a Levite (considered to be the most holy and compassionate people of the time), ignored the injured man. They passed by on the other side of the road, avoiding him and neglecting their obligation to help. The rest of this story was intended by God to shock the readers. It was meant to arouse the obligation to be merciful, because, as you may know, the hero of Jesus' story turns out to be a Samaritan. The people who originally heard Jesus tell the story would have expected the Samaritan to be the "bad guy." Samaritans were despised by the Israelites. And the Samaritans were none too fond of the Israelites either. But it is the Samaritan who stops immediately to render aid to the dying man. The Samaritan takes the injured man to an inn and covers all the man's expenses out of his own pocket. The implicit question asked by this parable is this: "If even a Samaritan can show mercy, what does that say about you?" Or to put it in more contemporary terms, "If even a bad guy sees the need to practice mercy, how much more should you?"

Some acts of mercy have received international acclaim. Mother Teresa bathed, fed, and sheltered dying men and women, many of whom were literally retrieved from the garbage heaps and scourged streets of Calcutta. She simply could not allow them to die "like animals on the street." Mother Teresa was awarded the Nobel Peace Prize for her humanitarian work in India and around the world.

Most acts of mercy never make the headlines. However, they do not go unnoticed. Unaware that she was Jewish, Dr. Renate Justin's new patient, at one point of her exam, began to spew her venomous and hideously evil views about the "Minderwertigen" (scum, low downs)—Jewish people who, as far as she was concerned, got what they deserved. According to Dr. Justin's patient, they deserved to be eliminated from the "Vaterland;" they deserved hard labor, starvation, and even the gas chamber. Dr. Justin began to gather the medical history on her new patient and discovered that she was German. Her husband had died fighting for Hitler; her son was a zealous member of the Hitler Youth; and, her role during the war was to supervise Jewish slave laborers.

How was Dr. Justin to explain to her venomous patient that she was Jewish? How could she tell her that she was, as her patient described it, "low-down scum," that her father had been in a concentration camp, and that many of her relatives died in the gas chambers? Dr. Justin rightfully felt as if she had been viciously assaulted, which led to a major dilemma. How could she possibly treat this person? How could she be a good physician to her? More than that, how could she be a compassionate, merciful physician? Her patient was suffering from chronic emphysema. She was losing the ability to breathe in and out. And yet, in that moment, she was reminded of the words of the Torah, "Let compassion breathe in and out of you, filling you with singing." These words reminded her that, even though her patient's behavior was worthy of judgment, she could not stifle her own obligation to show compassion. Amazingly, Dr. Justin offered to treat the new patient.

In each of these instances, people exercised their created capacity, as a bearer of God's image, to be compassionate to others, extending undeserved favor and mercy toward their well-being and peace. Brian Nichols did not deserve Ashley's favor; the Samaritan was not legally required to treat the Israelite that hated his race so deeply; and, Dr. Justin reserved the right to refuse treatment to any patient. Yet each person became an "angel of mercy," even to those who did not deserve it, even to those who hated and despised them.

## "It Is An Attribute Of God Himself."

This capacity to be merciful is an attribute of God given to you in the creation. But the exercise of this attribute is never easy. Simon Wiesenthal told the story of a dying man named Karl. Karl had been a Nazi. But on his deathbed he sought Wiesenthal's forgiveness for his personal involvement in the mass murder of thousands of Jews imprisoned in Polish concentration camps. This begs the question, how would you respond to Karl's death-bed confession and plea to "die in peace"? Would you show mercy to the dying German soldier? Would you treat the venomous German patient? Would you show mercy to the man who raped and killed your ten-year-old daughter? Would you show mercy to the young junior executive that made a ten million dollar mistake? Would you extend mercy to the driver who unexpectedly and abruptly cut in front of you in heavy traffic? The exercise of mercy is never easy. It takes time—oftentimes, courage—to claim, cultivate, and steward this created leadership attribute.

There is no better example of mercy than the Author of

mercy, God Himself. God is merciful. God is kind, loving, patient, and slow to anger. God bestows numerous blessings that people do not deserve, or for that matter, recognize and appreciate. The Bible is rich with wonderful examples of God's immeasurable mercy:

> For you, O Lord, are good and forgiving, abounding in steadfast love to all who call upon you.
>
> Psalm 86:5 (ESV)

> The LORD is merciful and gracious; slow to anger and abounding in steadfast love.
>
> Psalm 103:8 (ESV)

> Let us then with confidence draw near to the throne of grace, that we may receive mercy and find grace to help in time of need.
>
> Hebrews 4:16 (ESV)

> He saved us, not because of works done by us in righteousness, but according to his own mercy, by the washing of regeneration and renewal of the Holy Spirit.
>
> Titus 3:5 (ESV)

> Blessed be the God and Father of our Lord Jesus Christ! According to his great mercy, he has caused us to be born again to a living hope through the resurrection of Jesus Christ from the dead, to an inheritance that is imperishable, undefiled, and unfading, kept in heaven for you…
>
> I Peter 1:3–4 (ESV)

Sometimes, God extends His mercy toward people who are suffering and helpless like the sick, blind, lame, dead, hungry, childless, those trapped in the belly of a great fish, or to those who come face to face with wild beasts and giants. But there is much more to God's mercy than just His tender love and compassion toward those facing desperate straights. God often shows His mercy toward those who completely and utterly do not deserve His attention. The Bible tells that all people have sinned—that the penalty for that sin is death—and that everyone deserves God's justice and wrath. However, in His incomparable and loving mercy, God treats you better than you deserve. This punishment—this wrath—was poured out on Christ at Calvary. You deserve death—but received mercy. This is called "grace." Indeed, God's mercy is wonderfully expressed in the Blue Letter Bible,

> God has demonstrated (mercy) in abundance with respect to mankind. We from nearly the beginning of our existence have deserved nothing but wrath; having sinned and fallen short of eternal life in glory, we can do nothing to commend ourselves to or defend ourselves before God. But thankfully, God has been so amazing in His mercy. Over and against merely having the mercy to allow us to live out our miserable lives without destroying us instantly, God has chosen us to greatness and glory by the hand of His Son. The believer finds himself in Christ and enjoys full well the fruits of God's mercy. [59]

William Shakespeare captured the essence of this created attribute of mercy in his comedy, *The Merchant of Venice* (1597?) The villain is the moneylender, Shylock. Antonio, the protagonist, has defaulted on a loan. Shylock, who is offended and wounded, is not only seeking repayment, he is also out for vengeance. So, in payment for his loan, he demands a literal pound of Antonio's flesh. Shylock's heart is hard and becomes incapable of extending any mercy toward Antonio. In Act 4, Scene 1, Portia, the heroine disguised as a lawyer, speaks these famous words to Shylock as the court gathers to render judgment in this pivotal scene:

The quality of mercy is not strain'd,
It droppeth as the gentle rain from heaven
Upon the place beneath: it is twice blest;
It blesseth him that gives and him that takes:
'Tis mightiest in the mightiest: it becomes
The thronèd monarch better than his crown;
His *sceptre* shows the force of temporal power,
The attribute to awe and majesty,
Wherein doth sit the dread and fear of kings;
But *mercy* is above this sceptred sway;
It is enthronèd in the hearts of kings,
It is an attribute of God himself;
And earthly pow'r doth then show likest God's
When mercy seasons justice. Therefore, Jew,
Though justice be thy plea, consider this,
That, in the course of justice, none of us
Should see salvation: we do pray for mercy;
And that same prayer doth teach us all to render
deeds of mercy. [60]

Portia tried to persuade Shylock that mercy is as much of a benefit to the one who grants it as it is to the one who receives it, pleading, "It blesseth him that gives and him that takes," emphasizing, "It is an attribute of God himself."

## Merciful Leadership

There are two dimensions of the attribute of mercy, both perfectly mirrored in God Himself. The first is reflected in God's characteristic kindness toward those who are helpless, suffering, and in misery. It is out of God's mercy that He both observes and rescues those who are in need. He intercedes for the weak, the disabled, and the powerless. He heals the sick and thwarts the oppressor. He delivers the afflicted. He helps the poor and imprisoned. And He is known as the God who defends both the widow and the orphan. God simply delights in His mercy: "Who is a God like you, pardoning iniquity and passing over transgression for the remnant of his inheritance? He does not retain his anger forever, because he delights in steadfast love" (Micah 7:18, ESV). Little wonder that the Apostle Paul would tell the Christians in Ephesus,

> But God, being rich in mercy, because of the great love with which he loved us, even when we were dead in our trespasses, made us alive together with Christ—by grace you have been saved—and raised us up with him and seated us with him in the heavenly places in Christ Jesus, so that in the coming ages he might show the immeasurable riches of his grace in kindness toward us in Christ Jesus.
>
> Ephesians 2:4–7 (ESV)

It is this type of mercy that God extends to His image bearers, that compels them to extend mercy to the homeless, the orphans, the prisoners, those born with birth defects, those suffering from dementia or AIDS. It is this type of mercy that compels leaders to treat their employees as image bearers of God—not like another piece of machinery.

Yet, there is a much deeper and fuller meaning to God's mercy. His supreme act of mercy is delivering all of His creation from sin through the death and resurrection of His Son, Jesus Christ. To understand this dimension to God's mercy, you must grab hold of a deeper meaning to "mercy." Mercy is demonstrated when that which is deserved is withheld to the benefit of the object of the mercy. Since Adam and Eve sinned, you have deserved nothing less than the full wrath of God. You are a vile sinner. Not one person is righteous. You have fallen short of God's glory and deserve nothing less than God's full wrath and eternal punishment. Yet, because of God's rich mercy, you have been chosen for greatness and glory in and through Jesus Christ, God's Son. Short of God's mercy, you are completely and utterly without hope.

> He saved us, not because of works done by us in righteousness, but according to his own mercy, by the washing of regeneration and renewal of the Holy Spirit.
>
> Titus 3:5 (ESV)

> Blessed be the God and Father of our Lord Jesus Christ! According to his great mercy, he has caused us to be born again to a living hope through the resurrection of Jesus Christ from the dead.
>
> I Peter 1:3 (ESV)

## Practicing Merciful Leadership

Let's go one step further. Yes, God is merciful. But you are to be merciful just as God is merciful: "Be merciful, even as your Father is merciful" (Luke 6:36, ESV). Just as God acted in response to the plight of His children, you also are to act mercifully toward those who are in need—especially to those who, in your mind, do not deserve it. After all, God loved you even while you were His enemy. Responding to the needs of others is your opportunity to cultivate this created attribute. It is your opportunity to actively bear God's image—to be like your Creator and Father. Jesus affirmed this truth so simply—yet so powerfully to His disciples on a mountainside, "Blessed are the merciful, for they shall receive mercy" (Matthew 5:7, ESV).

Leaders are merciful. Mercy is a created leadership attribute. Effective leaders are often called upon to graciously and actively extend undeserved favor and mercy toward the well-being and peace of others. As such it becomes a core leadership trait. As a leader in your home, church, workplace, and community, how have you exercised this key leadership attribute this past week? Claiming this attribute begins by remembering that it is because of God's rich mercy that you are able to enjoy extending mercy to others. You fill the earth with the glory of God by reflecting this God-given attribute, mercy, to God and to your neighbors in everything you do and every place you go—home, work, church, and community. You are to extend mercy, as created leaders, to every one you encounter.

Portia understood this as she stood before Shylock. Speaking of mercy she pleaded,

> It is an attribute of God himself; and earthly pow'r doth then show likest God's when mercy seasons justice. We do pray for mercy. And that same prayer doth teach us all to render the deeds of mercy.

The practice of mercy identifies you with God. The practice

of mercy marks you as an effective leader. Your practice of mercy fills the earth with God's glory.

## Cultivating Merciful Leadership

Reclaim, cultivate, and steward this leadership attribute, mercy, in every arena of your life. Begin by completing the "Personal Reflection" exercise at the end of this chapter. Take time to thoughtfully and intentionally reflect on each question before recording your responses. Continue to invest quality time in responding to each question. Then complete the "Cultivating Your Created Leadership Capacity" exercise also found at the end of this chapter. This exercise will help you think through how best to apply merciful leadership in each one of your major life roles and spheres of influence. Remember, like God, you are called upon to be actively gracious and compassionate toward the well-being and peace of others through acts of favor and mercy—even to those who do not desire or deserve it.

You are merciful. You are a leader. This is the truth about leadership! This is the *Genesis Principle of Leadership*.

# Personal Reflection

*Leaders Are Merciful*

- Leadership is reclaiming and cultivating your God-given, created attributes. What specific action steps will you take to develop this leadership trait: Merciful?

- What does it mean that God is merciful?

- List three ways in which God has been merciful to you:

- List some specific actions you can take to be merciful to others:

- Which action will you implement this week?

- To whom?

- What result(s) do you expect from taking this action?

- Take a few moments—now—to pray about this action.

- In what way(s) could you help someone in your family, workplace, or community to claim and cultivate this leadership attribute in his life?

- Cultivate this created leadership trait by completing the "Cultivating Your Leadership Attributes" exercise on the next page.

## Cultivating Your Created Leadership Capacity

Leadership is the lifelong pursuit of claiming and cultivating your God-created attributes.

1. Select a Life Role (e.g. Leader, Spouse, Parent, Worker, Neighbor, etc.).

2. List the key Duties and Responsibilities of that Life Role.

3. Then design and list specific Action Steps that will enable you to steward this leadership attribute.

## Cultivating Merciful Leadership

As a leader you are called upon to be actively gracious and compassionate toward the well-being and peace of others through acts of favor and mercy—even to those who do not desire or deserve it.

# Life Role:

_____

| Duties/Responsibilities: | Leadership is Action: |
|---|---|

1. _____

2. _____

3. _____

4. _____

5. _____

6. _____

7. _____

*What you do with what you know is what Christian knowing is all about.* (Os Guinness)

# Leaders are Faithful

As a leader you entrust your life, well-being, and soul to the faithful and true Creator. Similarly, others acknowledge you as trustworthy and reliable as you faithfully do your work and good deeds. In this same way, you unreservedly view others as worthy of your trust, steadfastly relying upon them for the completion of the work.

## Hear This Now! I Will Come For You!

"Hear this now! I will come for you!" Westley smiles at her, Buttercup smiles too, throws her arms tightly around him. They kiss.

It's at this point in the movie, *The Princess Bride*, where the exasperated grandson (played by the youth actor, Fred Savage) interrupts his grandfather (played by Peter Falk) who is reading him a storybook and asks, "Is this a kissing book?"

You remember this wonderful fairytale don't you—the classic movie, *The Princess Bride*, directed by Rob Reiner? Swordplay—Torture—Revenge—Sea monsters—Mammoth rodents—Breathtaking chases—Narrow escapes—Miracles—A beautiful princess—An evil prince—True love—and, oh yes, some kissing! I'm certain that my grandchildren have seen this movie a hundred times. They can flawlessly recite every single line. Yet, like our children and grandchildren, we never tire of seeing this enchanting tale of adventure and true love.

In this story, Buttercup, the young farm maiden, and Westley (or "farm boy" as Buttercup affectionately called him) discover they are helplessly in love. But Westley has no money for a wedding. So, he decides to leave the farm in search of his fortune far across the sea. In a touching scene, Westley and Buttercup are standing at the gate to the farm embracing each other:

> BUTTERCUP: "I fear I'll never see you again, Westley."
>
> WESTLEY: "Of course you will."
>
> BUTTERCUP: "But what if something happens to you?"
>
> WESTLEY: "Hear this now! I will come for you!"[61]

He smiles at her, she smiles too, throws her arms so tightly around him. They kiss. Then as Westley walks away, Buttercup watches him go in search of his fortune.

But Westley never reached his destination. Time passed: scaling the Cliffs of Insanity—battling rodents of gargantuan size—facing torture in the Pit of Despair—and more. Buttercup feared that Westley had died.

But Westley did not die. He did return for Buttercup—just as he promised.

> WESTLEY: I told you, "I would always come for you." Why didn't you wait for me?
>
> BUTTERCUP: Well ... you were dead.

**WESTLEY:** Death cannot stop true love. All it can do is delay it for a while.

**BUTTERCUP:** I will never doubt again.

**WESTLEY:** There will never be a need.

And now, they kiss; it's a tender kiss, loving and gentle. Westley did what he said he would do. He was faithful.

## Unwavering Leadership

You were created to be faithful. As a bearer of God's image, you are to entrust your life, well-being, and soul to the faithful and true Creator. Similarly, others should acknowledge you as trustworthy and reliable as you faithfully do your work and good deeds. And in the same way, you are to view others as worthy of your trust and steadfastly rely upon them for the completion of the work.

There are three distinctive features to this crucial leadership attribute, faithful. First, as a leader, you must entrust your life, soul, well-being, and future to the true and faithful Creator. This must be done simply, completely, and without wavering. Why? Because the Bible tells us, "Let us hold fast the confession of our hope without wavering, for he who promised is faithful" (Hebrews 10:23, ESV). In other words, God is constant, reliable, and trustworthy. He can be counted on—so much so that among His names are the titles "Faithful" and "True" (Revelation 19:11, ESV). As a result, God deserves your full acceptance and confidence—nothing more; nothing less. Yes, there is a sense in which this is a passive trust. In other words, there is nothing in and of yourself that merits this attribute in God. There is nothing you can do but to simply rely upon the Creator who promised and is as good as His word. He has given you glorious and hope-filled promises, and has always shown Himself to be true to His promises—each and every time.

But there is also an active dimension to your complete and unwavering (though passive) trust in God. Because you place your trust and hope in the One who makes and keeps His promises, you can act. You must toil and strive to do what He expects of a faithful person. If you are faith-filled (that is, if you are active in your belief in, and trust of, God), you will joyously and passionately pursue deeds and works consistent with that faith. If you believe God is real, then you have to believe that His opinion of your character and conduct matters. And if He is truly God, His bidding and His wishes for your conduct should be your highest concern. Indeed, such an active, faith-filled trust appears to be what underlies the Apostle John's words when he encouraged his friend, Gaius, by saying, "I have no greater joy than to hear that my children are walking in the truth. Beloved, it is a *faithful thing you do* in all your efforts for these brothers" (III John: 5, ESV). In other words, John is excited, overjoyed, to find Gaius and others doing something with the truth that was revealed to them.

Being faithful is more than intellectual assent. True faith is a thing you do. Others should find you, as a bearer of God's image, to be constant, reliable, trustful, and one who can be counted on. Like Westley in *The Princess Bride*, you should do what you said you would do—you should do what you have been asked to do. As a leader, you must reflect the faithfulness of God by showing yourself to be faithful.

## The Naked Voice of God

Secondly, faithful leadership acknowledges that all people are made in the image of God. Therefore, leaders view others as worthy of trust. Effective leaders rely upon others for the completion of the work of filling the earth with God's glory. Effective leaders assign and delegate duties and responsibilities with a steadfast confidence in the willingness, ability, and trustworthiness of others to complete what they have agreed to do. Effective leaders believe that others can be counted upon.

Why not? What better role model do we have than God the Father, God the Son, and God the Holy Spirit? Each member of the Godhead is a perfect model of faithful. Faithfulness is a key characteristic of God the Father. Throughout history, God made promises to His people. Over and over again God kept those promises. He did what He said He would do: He promised Noah's family safety from the great flood, and they were delivered; He promised an old man with a barren wife that his descendants would outnumber the stars in the heaven, and then gave Abraham and Sarah a son; He promised Abraham, Isaac, and Jacob that their descendents would inherit a promised land, and then delivered His people out of bondage in Egypt and led them to the Promised Land; He told a shepherd boy that he would become a king, and then carried David onto the throne of Israel; He promised to bless David's descendants, and then gave wisdom to Solomon; He promised to send the seed of the woman who would crush the serpent's head, and then sent Jesus; He promised to solve the problem of a world broken by man's rebellion, and sacrificed the Lamb that took away the sins of the world; and, He promised to grant eternal life to His people, and He sent a Savior whose resurrection secures eternal life and His Spirit to lead us on this sanctifying journey. With every promise, God was true to His word. God kept his promises. He was faithful. He *is* faithful.

The ancients of old staked their lives and reputations on these promises. As Luther put it, these leaders believed and followed "the naked voice of God." Because of this faith: Abel was commended as a righteous man; Enoch was taken from this life without experiencing death; Noah became an heir of righteousness; Abraham became a father of all the faithful; Moses rescued his people from the tyranny of the Pharaoh; the walls of Jericho fell; and, Rahab was rescued. There are so many examples. As the writer of Hebrews put it,

> And what more shall I say? For time would fail me to tell of Gideon, Barak, Samson, Jephthah, of David and Samuel and the prophets—who through faith conquered kingdoms, enforced justice, obtained promises, stopped the mouths of lions, quenched the power of fire, escaped the edge of the sword, were made strong out of weakness, became mighty in war, put foreign armies to flight. Women received back their dead by resurrection. Some were tortured, refusing to accept release, so that they might rise again to a better life. Others suffered mocking and flogging, and even chains and imprisonment. They were stoned, they were sawn in two, and they were killed with the sword. They went about in skins of sheep and goats, destitute, afflicted, mistreated—of whom the world was not worthy—wandering about in deserts and mountains, and in dens and caves of the earth.
>
> Hebrews 11:32–38 (ESV)

All because of the faithfulness of the God who promised!

Faithfulness is a key characteristic of God the Son. His faithfulness was first observed when Joseph and Mary, fearing that their son was lost, found him three days later in the temple. Jesus seemed to be surprised that His parents were so distraught, "Didn't you know I must be in my Father's house?" (Luke 2:49, ESV). Jesus attested to His own faithfulness,

> For I have come down from heaven, not to do my own will but the will of him who sent me. And this is the will of him who sent me that I should lose nothing of all that he has given me, but raise it up on the last day.
>
> John 6:38 (ESV)

In the Garden of Gethsemane Jesus showed his faithfulness to the ghastly task that was ahead of Him, "Not my will, but yours be done" (Matthew 26:42, ESV). In the book of John, chapter 10, Jesus faithfully promised that He would not lose any of his sheep. In chapter 14, Jesus reminded His disciples of His faithfulness and trustworthiness, "If it were not so, I would have told you." (John 14:2, ESV). In the book of John, chapter 15, Jesus promised that whatever we ask in His name He would be faithful to give it to us. And then of course, Jesus proved His trustworthiness by saying He would be raised from the dead and then actually arose. Just as God the Father is faithful, so, too, God the Son, Jesus, is faithful to all that He has promised. What He has promised is certain. It has and will come to pass. We can count on His promises. We can count on Him to deliver. Jesus is faithful.

Faithfulness is a key characteristic of God the Holy Spirit. The Holy Spirit, who is the same in substance and equal in power and glory with God the Father and God the Son, is also completely faithful and trustworthy. The Holy Spirit is faithful in uniting you, lastingly, to Christ; faithfully equipping you, God's child, with gifts that enable you to grow the church into unity, maturity, and strength; and faithfully interceding for you "with groanings which cannot be uttered" (Romans 8: 26–27, ESV). The Holy Spirit is faithful, trustworthy, and reliable. The Holy Spirit is the guarantor of your salvation, granting hope in eternal life. The Holy Spirit gives you the ability to serve the living God. The Holy Spirit enables you to resist the author of evil, Satan himself (Hebrew 9:14). The Holy Spirit is your faithful companion on the journey of life.

## Faithful Leadership

Since faithfulness is a key characteristic of God the Father, God the Son, and God the Holy Spirit, faithfulness is a key characteristic of God's servants, His leaders. God created you to be faithful and to live faithfully. In fact, God will judge you regarding your faithfulness: "I thank him who has given me strength, Christ Jesus our Lord, because he judged me faithful, appointing me to his service..." (I Timothy 1:12, ESV) Your obligation to be faithful is assumed when God refers to you as a "good and faithful servant" (Matthew 25:21, ESV), a "faithful servant" (Matthew 25:23, ESV), a "faithful minister in the Lord" (Ephesians 6:21, ESV), and as a "faithful minister of Christ" (Colossians 1:7, ESV). Faithfulness is a characteristic of effective leaders. Leaders entrust their life, well-being, and soul to the faithful and true Creator. Consequently, others acknowledge leaders as trustworthy and reliable as they faithfully do their work and good deeds. In the same way, leaders unreservedly view others as worthy of trust and steadfastly rely upon them for the completion of the work.

Faithful leaders lead with their heart, head, hands, honor, hospitality, humbleness, and happiness. First, leaders possess confident, compassionate, and courageous hearts. Typically, this is a quiet, yet compelling, confidence in the One who not only created the universe, but fulfills the eternal decrees of the Lord of that universe. Leaders have compassion for the people who were also created in the image of God and possess divinely appointed niches in fulfilling God's plan. Leaders are courageous—fully engaging every arena of life, personal and professional, with no fear. They possess the conviction, like John Wesley, that "Until my work is complete I am immortal." In other words, until the work that you came to earth to do is completed—every tiny detail—God will allow no harm to befall you. Nothing will interfere with the completion of your divinely appointed work. You've observed and admire people like this—confident, compassionate, and courageous. Names and faces come to mind, don't they? What about Mother Teresa, for example?

Faithful leaders lead with their heads in rational, reliable, and responsible ways. Because leaders are image bearers of the Creator, they are rational. They have the created capacity to make wise, fair, and sensible decisions. Leaders are reliable. They can be counted upon to be consistent, fair, and reasonable in their decisions and judgments. And leaders not only take and own full responsibility for their work, but are also willing to share this work with others.

Faithful leaders lead with their hands. In other words, leaders are action-oriented. They are connecting, challenging, and changing the circumstances around them. They do not view themselves as a "victim" of their circumstances, nor do they stand passively on the sidelines wondering, "What just happened?" Life is a contact sport for faithful leaders. Leaders apply their created attributes by entering and engaging every arena of their personal and professional lives. Leaders challenge and confront, boldly at times, every corner of culture for God and for good.

Faithful leaders lead with honor. Contrary to the conventional wisdom of today's modern culture, leaders do have a moral center. That is, effective leaders have developed a set of principled and ethical core values that direct their personal and professional lives. Therefore, faithful leaders are trustworthy. Leaders are honest; leaders tell the whole truth—all of the time; and leaders are reliable—they do what they said they would do when they said they would do it. Faithful leaders trust others as image bearers of God and, therefore, consider them to be reliable and trustworthy. Or to put it more simply, they have high expectations of others.

Faithful leaders are hospitable. They are approachable. Their demeanor invites and welcomes the thoughts, ideas, and concerns of others. Simply stated, faithful leaders are easy to talk to. Leaders are attentive, alert, and responsive; they give their undivided attention to others. They actively and attentively listen to what is being said and connect with the communicator. Leaders are amiable, interacting with others in warm, friendly, and lighthearted ways.

Faithful leaders are humble. This is not a false humility so often used by some to manipulate others (I actually attended a workshop once where we were coached on how to make others believe we were humble). Rather, there is a genuine inner calmness in leaders. They are "calm, cool, and collected." Humble leaders have a distinguishing unruffled, serene, tranquil, and composed demeanor. Seldom do they become ruffled and disquieted—not even in their inner-most being. Leaders reveal an inner calmness that calms others in the midst of unsettling situations—often by simply walking into the situation—without having to say or do anything other than just being present.

Faithful leaders are happy. Deep inside they are content, satisfied, and at peace regardless of their circumstances. They are not defeated, depressed, nor distraught. Happy leaders are, in fact, comfortable and at peace. They are, truthful, cheerful, joyful, and in good spirits. Consequently, faithful leaders are encouraging. That is, their cheerfulness is contagious. They have the ability to encourage others and lead them out of their defeated mindset into a more positive frame—energizing them to greater work and impact.

## Cultivating Faithful Leadership

Reclaim, cultivate, and steward this important leadership attribute, faithful, in every arena of your life. Once again, complete the "Personal Reflection" exercise that follows. Take time to thoughtfully and intentionally reflect on each question before recording your responses. Continue to invest quality time in responding to each question. Then complete the "Cultivating Your Created Leadership Capacity." This exercise will help you think through how best to apply faithful leadership in each one of your major life roles and spheres of influence. Remember, you are faithful. You are to entrust your life, well-being, and soul to the faithful and true Creator. Similarly, others should acknowledge you as trustworthy and reliable as you faithfully do your work and good deeds. In this same way, unreservedly view others as worthy of your trust, relying upon them for the completion of the work.

You are faithful. You are a leader. This is the truth about leadership! This is the *Genesis Principle of Leadership*.

## Personal Reflection

### *Leaders Are Faithful*

- Leadership is reclaiming and cultivating your God-given, created attributes. What specific action steps will you take to develop this leadership trait: Faithful?

- What does it mean that God is faithful?

- List three ways in which God has been faithful to you:

- List some specific actions you can take to be faithful to others:

- Which action will you implement this week?

- To whom?

- What result(s) do you expect from taking this action?

- Take a few moments—now—to pray about this action.

- In what way(s) could you help someone in your family, workplace, or community to claim and cultivate this leadership attribute in his life?

- Cultivate this created leadership trait by completing the "Cultivating Your Created Leadership Capacity" exercise on the next page.

## Cultivating Your Created Leadership Capacity

Leadership is the lifelong pursuit of claiming and cultivating your God-created attributes.

1. 1) Select a Life Role (e.g. Leader, Spouse, Parent, Worker, Neighbor, etc.).
2. 2) List the key Duties and Responsibilities of that Life Role.
3. 3) Then design and list specific Action Steps that will enable you to steward this leadership attribute.

## Cultivating Faithful Leadership

As a leader you entrust your life, well-being, and soul to the faithful and true Creator. Similarly, others acknowledge you as trustworthy and reliable as you faithfully do your work and good deeds. In this same way, you unreservedly view others as worthy of your trust, steadfastly relying upon them for the completion of the work.

# Life Role:

_____

| Duties/Responsibilities: | Leadership is Action: |
|---|---|
| 1. | |
| 2. | |
| 3. | |
| 4. | |
| 5. | |
| 6. | |
| 7. | |

*What you do with what you know is what Christian knowing is all about.* (Os Guinness)

# Leaders Are Interdependent

As a leader you are totally and dynamically reliant upon God and your fellow human beings for your well-being and continued existence. Nonetheless, you remain irreducibly distinctive, independent, and irreplaceable with even greater individual capacity, influence, and significance, finding the center of your existence and significance in God and others.

## "I Won't Dance"

Some people collect stamps; some collect rare coins; others collect antiques or baseball cards. I collect experiences. My life's album is a treasure chest of incredible, thrilling, "once-in-a-lifetime" adventures. A few experiences have been life-changing quests. I must warn you! I am armed with pictures to prove it! Gratefully, I continue to have a zeal for adding even more pages to my collection of adventures.

However, there is one experience I have no desire whatsoever to add to my collection. I won't dance! I am of the same mind as the English composer, Sir Arnold Box, who encouraged that one "should make a point of trying every experience once...except...folk dancing."[62] Whew! What a relief! I am eager for my next adventure—but not dancing!

Sarah, my wife, is one of those tormented women described by Groucho Marx, who once quipped, "Wives are people who feel they don't dance enough." She suffers great anguish because I won't dance with her. Every fiber of her being yearns, desires, even aches, to waltz, polka, salsa, square dance, clog, even bunny hop at wedding receptions. But I won't even slow dance. I admit, it grieves me to see the hurt in her eyes—but I just won't dance.

Now don't misunderstand me. I don't have any moral or religious convictions against dancing. I have to confess, though, that in my effort to find any flimsy excuse to avoid dancing, I have used, abused, perhaps, the words of the seventeenth century Puritan Pamphleteer, William Prynne, who wrote in 1622:

> Dancing is, for the most part, attended with many amorous smiles, wanton compliments, unchaste kisses, scurrilous songs and sonnets, effeminate music, lust-provoking attire, ridiculous love pranks, all which savor only of sensuality, of raging fleshly lusts. Therefore it is to be wholly abandoned of all good Christians.[63]

I'm sure that by now you are thinking that I am the perfect prude. So let me shine more light on the matter. I simply can't dance. Every self-conscious fiber of my being rises to the surface. I feel exposed and naked. I feel that every single eye in the universe is riveted on me—snickering at me as I trip and stumble and jerk around the dance floor. My joints and muscles lock up. I end up standing, rigidly, in the middle of the dance floor—completely embarrassed and humiliated. It is at this moment that the words of the rock group, Genesis, play over and over and over again in my head:

> I can't dance, I can't talk.
> The only thing about me is the way I walk.
> I can't dance, I can't sing
> I'm just standing here selling everything.

## An Irreducible Dynamic

Ironically, though, I enjoy watching others dance. I enjoy attending the ballet. I've even purchased front row seats to Michael Flately's *Lord of the Dance* three times, so that I could fully experience, albeit vicariously, the classic tale of good versus evil, played out by perfect precision dancing, dramatic original music, colorful costumes, and state-of-the-art production techniques. I am amazed by the virtuosity of the dancers, who, it is estimated, complete 151,200 taps per show. I wonder how they can never seem to miss a beat. By the way, who had the time, energy, and keenness of eyesight to count 151,200 taps?

Indeed, there is indescribable beauty and elegance in watching a dancer reveal her soul through the movements of her body—dancing, as choreographer George Balanchine said, "…not because she wants to—but because she has to." Nothing is more inspiring than watching people perform with energy, grace, and technical precision.

Yet, something more moving, more stirring occurs when dancers discover that they are not just good dancers because of their individual ability and technique, rather they become incredible dancers because of their passionate, soulish, interconnectedness with the other dancer(s). A dancer may be technically perfect individually, but when a dancer is partnered with someone else, when the dancers rely on each other to express a shared message, something more powerful, more graceful, more expressive, and more magnificent is created. Fred Astaire was a wonderful dancer, but when he danced with Ginger Rogers, it was magical!

Such dancers are totally and dynamically reliant upon each other for their continued being and existence. The result is an artistic expression far surpassing anything they could create and perform individually. Such dancers have greater individual capacity, effect, and significance because they are mutually and dynamically interdependent upon one another. Simply stated, they are better together! As author Catherine Mowry LaCugna put it:

> There is a mutual interanimation, dynamic reciprocity, and unsurpassable beauty between the dancers that can only be understood as an irreducible relational dynamic that simultaneously affirms both individuality and mutuality. [64]

Now don't tell Sarah, but deep down inside, I long to dance like this. Yes! I would dance, if only I could dance like this. Secretly, I harmonize with the French dramatist, director, theatre manager and actor, Moliere':

> All the ills of mankind, all the tragic misfortunes that fill the history books, all the political blunders, all the failures of the great leaders have arisen merely from a lack at dancing. (1622)

## Lord of the Dance

There is a magnificent and transcendent picture of this kind of interdependence in the Godhead, the Holy Trinity. The early church fathers used the word *perichoresis* to describe the interdependent relationship of God the Father, God the Son, and God the Holy Spirit. Interestingly, this word, *perichoresis,* is the root word for "dance." *Perichoresis* speaks about a deep interpenetrating relationship, a mutual indwelling, and a reciprocal interrelationship between the members of the Holy Trinity. The Trinity is significantly more than three distinct people who learned how to get along simply because they attended a team-building seminar together. There is a mutual relationship that is so deep and so complete that each person is completely in the other two—yet without coalescence, without losing any individual distinctiveness. God the Father becomes even more distinctive as He completely interpenetrates God the Son and God the Holy Spirit; God the Son becomes even more distinctive as He completely interpenetrates God the Father and God the Holy Spirit; and, God the Holy Spirit becomes even more distinctive as He completely interpenetrates God the Father and God the Son.

Glimpses of this perichoretic model are found in the Scriptures:

> Do you not believe that I am in the Father and the Father is in me? The words that I say to you I do not speak on my own authority, but the Father who dwells in me does his works.
>
> John 14:10 (ESV)

Dynamically, each member of the Trinity becomes individually more distinctive as each one becomes more interconnected with the others. Their unique individuality and roles emerge as they become more interconnected and interdependent. Sinclair Ferguson, the renowned Scottish preacher and theologian, defined this interdependent dynamic this way:

No language can define, far less exhaust, the meaning of these relationships. The Spirit would help the disciples to grasp the intimacy of the Son's indwelling by and of the Father—what earlier theologians called circumincessio or perichoresis, the mutual indwelling of one another by the persons of the Trinity, the 'dancing around' of each other in which the mutual harmony and love among the persons of the Trinity find expression. [65]

## Teach Me How to Twirl and How to Move

There is a stunning depiction of this deep and intimate relationship in the members of the Godhead. Jesus invited us into that very same, dancing, relationship:

> I do not ask for these only, but also for those who will believe in me through their word, that they may all be one, just as you, Father, are in me, and I in you, that they also may be in us, so that the world may believe that you have sent me. The glory that you have given me I have given to them, that they may be one even as we are one. I in them and you in me, that they may become perfectly one, so that the world may know that you sent me and loved them even as you loved me.
>
> John 17: 20–23 (ESV)

Andrew Stephen Damick captured this perichoretic portrait so wonderfully in his poem, *Perichoresis*. Again, don't tell Sarah, but these words make me want to join the dance:

## Perichoresis

O elegant and gentle Leader of the dance,
we do not know the meaning of each step
nor how to rightly turn this way or hold this pose.
Each spinning step or angled movement's twist
does sometimes give us vertigo here where we stand;
this mystery of how the rhythm's pulse
and how the music's lilt are tuned to only You
has caught us up, and we are overwhelmed.

O grace-filled, grace-bestowing Leader of the dance,
please teach me how to twirl and how to move;
please teach me how the song pervades each dancer's form,
these dancers who have learned to dance with You
throughout the ages of the song, the holy song
You sang in ages past to Abraham,
to Isaac and to Jacob and his Hebrew seed:
Now sing to me and give me, too, this life.

O Leader of the dance, this perfect partnership
of Leader and of led, of God and man,
this Incarnation's holy dance we see in You,
You now invite us to accompany.
This awesome dance, a truly cosmic synergy,
the interpenetration of us men
with Deity—with Trinity!—the universe
beholds and stands amazed and bows its head.

O holy Leader of this cosmic circling dance,
the union of both man and God is here
and imaged in the holy mystery of life
conjoined, a woman and a man conjoined.
He takes Your role as gentle leader, she as Church,

she follows him, and he must die for her;
their dance together joins the dance eternal now,
and in that human dance we see our God.

O Holy Trinity, Your dance eternal now
descends on us and consecrates our own,
the revelation here as Body and as Blood;
herein we taste the God become a man,
and men become as gods as David prophesied.
The Trinitarian rhythm has become
our own, to guide our dance, to grasp our hands and lead
us in the dance of stillness perfectly. [66]

What a magnificent picture of how you are to relate to others! Did you catch the last line? "The Trinitarian rhythm has become our own, to guide our dance, to grasp our hands and lead us in the dance of stillness perfectly." God created you in His image. As a bearer of His image, you, like each member of the Godhead, are interdependent. You were created with the capacity for a deep, mutual, interpenetrating, interdependent relationship with God and with others. You have been invited to the dance—even though you may not know how to dance. In this dance, you become even more distinctive in your responsibility to be a bearer of God's image.

## Independent Interdependence without Codependency

This interconnectedness is a remarkable picture of effective leadership. Contrary to popular belief, effective leaders are not hard-nosed, cigar-chomping, commandeering, uncaring, individualistic, take-charge, lone wolves. Effective leaders are interdependent. This is a difficult concept for the rugged, individualistic

American to accept, much less to put in practice. Leaders, true leaders, learned a long time ago that they can not be successful "doing it their way." Even so, there is more to effective leadership than simply learning how to get along with others by attending team-building seminars, implementing participative management teams, or keeping up with Japanese leadership models. Leaders truly understand that there is a complete, mutual, and dynamic reciprocity between all members of the team. It is this reciprocity that simultaneously increases organizational effectiveness while offering individuality and synergistic togetherness. Leadership is a perichoretic dance—a circle of shared life. It's not all about "me." It is independent interdependence without codependency.

The antiquated, 1960's, individualized, independent, lone-wolf approach to leadership is reflected in too many of the current top-selling books and articles on leadership. For example, on one popular website, *www.About.com,* John Reh identified the top three leadership books that, in his opinion, "best capture the ideas of leadership." About the book, *One-Minute Manager*[67] by Spencer Johnson and Kenneth H. Blanchard, Reh said, "This book is universal and timeless and will enable *you* to get more out of *your* life and more out of *your* people." Reh's second choice was *Executive Thinking: The Dream, The Vision, The Mission Achieved* by Leslie Kossoff.[68] Reh said this book dares executives "to dream and challenges *them* to take actions necessary to align *their* organizations with *their* dreams." In describing his third choice, *Leading Change* by John Kotter,[69] Reh said that this book laid out "...eight simple steps to show that *you* are the *one* responsible for making change happen." Each of Reh's endorsements placed the focus and emphasis on the central role of the individual leader. One can almost hear the refrain, "If it's up to me, it's up to me...and only me." I will "do it my way."

Sadly, Reh was correct—these three books do, in fact, capture the major emphasis in today's literature on individualistic models of leadership. Reh's "top picks," like so many other leadership books and articles being written today, completely miss the vital interdependent dimension to effective leadership. There is so much more to leadership than identifying individual traits and characteristics, learning how one can exercise power, or building participative management teams. These kinds of approaches, though popular, fall far short because they do not tap into the ultimate depth and reality of interdependence. You become a truly effective leader when you become interdependent upon the people you are leading. Effective leaders are interdependent.

## Pathetic Views of Leadership

Too many current notions about leadership are based upon pathetically undignified (i.e. mechanistic) views of personhood. There is little to no willingness to recognize that people have rational minds and that they observe, think, value, and make judgments. Rather, the human mind is viewed as nothing more than a machine. Therefore, these "machines" are to be managed in much the same way one would manage any machine. "Machines" can be programmed to work in particular ways—in accordance with prescribed, engineered specifications (i.e. policies).

Thankfully, this mechanistic approach to leadership has been shown to be outdated and ineffective. Nevertheless, the scientific approach to management continues to be the driving force behind many leadership strategies promoted by today's leadership gurus. Such depersonalizing approaches irresponsibly lead to the development of such things as policy manuals that attempt to force employees to perform tasks in narrowly prescribed, repeatable, machine-like fashion—all in the name of "efficiency." As one employee told me, "We are not paid to think around here."

Don't misunderstand me; policies are important. But, in my judgment, leadership by policy-making is dehumanizing and dangerous. Leading by policy-making is driven by the behavioristic philosophies discussed earlier in the book. Such philosophies tend toward the devaluing of the individual and the undervaluing of the dignity and worth of each person as an image bearer of God. There is little to no regard for how people think, perceive, value, or process the world around them. Though this approach to leadership is antiquated and unproductive, the pressures of volatile economic, political, and global competition perpetuate its use by the illusion of repeatable production, consistent output, or increased productivity. We are beginning to witness the negative consequences of its use. Even as production has increased, the quality of goods and services has suffered. But should we really be surprised that the quality of products and services decline when people are undervalued and treated like machines? Leading by policy making is the lowest form of human behavior.

## A Step Forward

Occasionally, there have been leadership models that recognize that people are something more than programmable machines—that acknowledge that people, in fact, can think, reason, and are capable of judging for themselves—that it is not necessary for them to check their thoughts, ideas, and feelings at the door when they arrive for work—and that they don't have to leave at the end of the day feeling like they have been treated like a number, or worse yet, a machine. In fact, their individual thoughts and feelings might actually prove valuable to the productivity and effectiveness of the organization. Japanese competitiveness and ingenuity prompted the rise to "quality management" or "participative management" team models, which allowed employees the opportunity for input into the improvement of products, goals, and the processes of the organization. This was an encouraging step forward. But the overall effectiveness of this approach to leadership was limited, and, in some cases, held in check by a pervasive and suspicious view of personhood. Very few innovative ideas posited by workers were actually accepted and implemented because these new approaches to leadership did not fit into the long-held, traditional corporate values or the views of the management.

## Level Three Leadership

James Clawson took leadership to a higher level in his book, *Level Three Leadership: Getting Below the Surface*. [70] Clawson argued that effective leadership must recognize that people are much more than programmable machines. People have an intricately developed, personal set of values, assumptions, beliefs, and expectations (i.e. VABEs). According to Clawson, workers do not check their VABEs at the door when they arrive at the workplace. People, like you and me, use their world and life views—their conceptual framework—to observe, describe, interpret, and make decisions about the world around them, and then act accordingly. Clawson said that because employees are, in fact, stakeholders and not machines, there must be a moral foundation to leadership that consists of four cornerstones: truth-telling, promise-keeping, fairness, and respect for each individual. What a remarkable leap from the mechanical and dehumanizing approaches to leadership still prevalent in the twenty-first century!

## Let's Kick It Up a Notch!

But there's more. In the words popularized by the cooking icon, Emeril Lagasse, "Let's kick it up a notch!" I want to take Clawson's "Level Three" notion to a higher level. Clawson's fourth cornerstone is "respect for the individual." Clawson said, "Respect for the individual means believing that all individuals have some intrinsic worth and should be treated accordingly with courtesy and kindness."[71] Clawson illustrates this with the common Buddhist greeting, "Namaste," interpreted as, "I respect the part of God that is within you." Clawson has it right—*almost.* People do have something "divine" within. Leaders should show respect for that "divinity." But I suggest that the traditional Christian view of "*imago Dei*" kicks the Buddhist notion of namaste up a notch—to a higher biblical view of leadership—*The Genesis Principle of Leadership.* You were carefully and purposefully created in God's image; you possess most of God's attributes; and, you are responsible to be a bearer of these attributes in every arena of your life—including the *Genesis Charge* to lead.

Though distorted by sin, every one of your co-workers and subordinates possesses, in equal portion and capacity, the created attributes of God. It is your moral responsibility, as a leader, to recognize, cultivate, and help each other steward these created leadership attributes. This is interdependence. This is the beginning of effective leadership.

Let me give you an example. *www.Google.com* is a company that has implemented some innovative leadership strategies based upon a higher view of the person. Some of Google's corporate policy is based upon such values such as: "You can make money without doing evil." "You can be serious without a suit." "Work should be challenging and the challenge should be fun." All Google engineers are encouraged to spend 20% of their work time on projects that interest them. Imagine that! Yet, some of Google's newer products and services, such as *Gmail, Google News,* and *Orkut,* originated from these independent endeavors. And the creativity and innovation at *www.Google.com* continues, including such things as lava lamps in the lobby, workout rooms, a massage room, recreation centers, fully stocked snack rooms scattered throughout the corporate headquarters (named "Googleplex") and a host of other amenities that encourages innovation and creativity.

## Cultivating Interdependent Leadership

It is crucial that you begin, today, to reclaim, cultivate, and steward this important leadership attribute. Begin by completing the "Personal Reflection" exercise that follows. Take time to thoughtfully and intentionally reflect on each question before recording your responses. Invest quality time in responding to each question. Then complete the "Cultivating Your Created Leadership Capacity." This exercise will help you think through how best to apply interdependent leadership in each one of your major life roles and spheres of influence. Remember, you are interdependent. You are totally and dynamically reliant upon God and your fellow human beings for your well-being and continued existence. Nonetheless, you remain irreducibly distinctive, independent, and irreplaceable with even greater individual capacity, influence, and significance, finding the center of your existence and significance in God and others.

You are interdependent. You are a leader. This is the truth about leadership. This is the *Genesis Principle of Leadership*.

## Personal Reflection

*Leaders Are Interdependent*

- Leadership is reclaiming and cultivating your God-given, created attributes. What specific action steps will you take to develop this leadership trait: *Interdependent?*

- What does it mean that God is interdependent?

- List three ways in which God has been interdependent with you:

- List some specific actions you can take to be interdependent with others:

- Which action will you implement this week?

- To whom?

- What result(s) do you expect from taking this action?

- Take a few moments—now—to pray about this action.

- In what way(s) could you help someone in your family, workplace, or community to claim and cultivate this leadership attribute in his life?

- Cultivate this created leadership trait by completing the "Cultivating Your Created Leadership Capacity" exercise on the next page.

## Cultivating Your Created Leadership Capacity

Leadership is the lifelong pursuit of claiming and cultivating your God-created attributes.

1. 1) Select a Life Role (e.g. Leader, Spouse, Parent, Worker, Neighbor, etc.).
2. 2) List the key Duties and Responsibilities of that Life Role.
3. 3) Then design and list specific Action Steps that will enable you to steward this leadership attribute.

## Cultivating Interdependent Leadership

As a leader you are totally and dynamically reliant upon God and your fellow human beings for your well-being and continued existence. Nonetheless, you remain irreducibly distinctive, independent, and irreplaceable with even greater individual capacity, influence, and significance, finding the center of your existence and significance in God and others.

## LIFE ROLE:

_____

Duties/Responsibilities:      Leadership is Action:

1. _____

2. _____

3. _____

4. _____

5. _____

6. _____

7. _____

*What you do with what you know is what Christian knowing is all about.* (Os Guinness)

# Leaders Are Generous

As a leader you possess the created capacity and responsibility to be generous as God is generous, dispensing the sacrificial generosity of God to those around you by being supremely and wastefully generous with your time, talent, and treasure.

## "Give Everything Away?"

"And how is it that this person has never given me one of her quilts?"

In their beautiful, award-winning, picture book, *The Quiltmaker's Gift*,[72] Jeff Brumbeau and Gail de Marcken tell the enchanting story of a very powerful and greedy king who, with the help of a little old quiltmaker, learned how to excel in the grace of giving.

In fact, this king was good, very good, at being greedy. Every Christmas and every birthday (which he celebrated twice each year) the king demanded that his subjects lavish astonishingly beautiful and magical gifts upon him. Oh how the king loved his possessions! He kept an accurate and detailed inventory of each one. From top to bottom, every nook and cranny of his castle was filled with the magnificent gifts he had received.

But the king was not happy. He never smiled. He was never satisfied. He kept looking for that one perfect gift that would finally make him happy.

One day the king learned about a quiltmaker who lived in her little cottage in the mountains—high above the clouds. Throughout the world, people said that this quiltmaker made the brightest and prettiest quilts that anyone had ever seen. Curiously, though, she never sold her quilts. People came from all over the world with pockets full of money to buy her magnificent quilts. Yet, no matter how hard they tried, she would not sell even one. No amount of gold or silver could change her mind. Instead, she always took her quilts to the town and gave them to the downtrodden and homeless. Then she would start another, and then another, only to give them away.

The king demanded one of these magnificent quilts. "And how is it that this person has never given me one of her quilts?" he bellowed. But the quiltmaker refused. Several times the king threatened her. But again and again the quiltmaker refused. On one occasion the king threw the quiltmaker into the cave of a hungry bear. On another occasion the king placed her on a tiny, deserted island. Still, the quiltmaker refused to give the king one of her extraordinary quilts.

Eventually, in desperation, the king shouted, "I give up! What must I do for you to give me a quilt?" In response, the quiltmaker finally promised to make the king a quilt, on one condition. He had to give away everything he owned to the poor. The king was stunned. Give away everything? Every one of his treasured gifts? What an absurd idea! The king dearly loved each and every one of his gifts. How could he possibly give them away? How could he even give one?

## The "Richest" One in the World

But finally, he gave in. He began ever so slowly at first. Starting with his smaller treasures, the king gave them away one by one. To his astonishment, he began to experience pleasure—not in receiving gifts—but in giving them away. Little by little he began to smile—and even laugh as he emptied his castle. Soon his happiness turned into a deep, satisfying joy. Even so, he could not understand how it was possible that he could experience such happiness by giving away his treasured possessions. But soon, the king was giving away his gifts by the wagonload. He excelled in the grace of giving, becoming overwhelmed with inexpressible joy.

It took years for the king to give away everything. He went everywhere. He gave everyone he saw a gift. Soon there was not a person in his kingdom who had not received a gift from him. What joy filled his soul as he traded his treasures for smiles!

Finally, tired, tattered, and torn, the weary king returned home—poor—with holes in the toes of his boots. He had traveled all over the world giving away his treasures. Nevertheless, his eyes glittered with joy and his laugh had grown wonderful and thunderous. At last, he was happy. Though poor, he felt like he was the richest person in the world.

The king kept his promise to the quiltmaker. He gave every one of his beautiful gifts away. And the quiltmaker kept her promise to the king and gave him one of the most beautiful quilts she had ever made. But the quiltmaker also kept her promise to herself—giving her quilts only to the poor. She stayed true to her calling; she excelled in the grace of giving.

Curiously, the king returned to the town only to give away his beautiful quilt to one he found shivering in the cold of night.

The quiltmaker continued to make her magnificent quilts. From time to time the king would go to the quiltmaker's little cottage high above the clouds and at night, take them down to the town, and give them to the poor and downtrodden. As this wonderful parable ends, it is said that the king was "never happier than when he was giving something away."

What a wonderfully woven story of generosity! Yet the story of God's generosity is even more compelling! Each member of the Godhead gave, and continues to give, in unsurpassing abundance. God the Father created and sustains the universe; God the Son graciously gave His life that you might live an eternally abundant life; and God the Holy Spirit equips you with divinely originated abilities that enable you to play a unique and strategic role in transforming every corner of culture for God and for good. Supreme generosity is at the very core of God's nature.

It is an attribute that God gave to you. In other words, you were created to be gloriously generous. It is part of your created nature and divine responsibility, as a bearer of God's image, to be supremely generous with your time, talent, and treasure. Yes, the story of the greedy king who learned to excel in the grace of giving is a wonderful example. But what better example can be found than in the supreme, inexpressible generosity of God, the King of Kings?

## Gloriously and Wastefully Generous Leadership

Excelling in the grace giving is not an abstract, dusty, theological notion. God is exuberantly, cheerfully, and lavishly generous. God's acts of generosity are transformative. God's generosity is real. God's generosity changes things. God loves to give. In his masterful collection of daily devotional poems, *The Diary of an Old Soul,* the Victorian poet, novelist, and Christian fantasy writer, George MacDonald (1824—1905), described God's generosity as "gloriously wasteful." In his poem for March 2, MacDonald wrote, "Gloriously wasteful, O my Lord, art Thou."[73]

God created you to be gloriously and wastefully generous. The generosity of your time, talent, and treasure also changes things. In fact, in the final analysis, it may be the only thing that ever changes things. And like the greedy king, you too will learn that you are the true benefactor of your own generosity. Like the greedy king, you, too, will experience great joy and fulfillment as you learn to excel in the grace of giving. Furthermore, God takes great joy and delight in watching His people cheerfully and lavishly—even wastefully—bestow gifts of their time, talent, and treasure in changing people and the world about them. God gives cheerfully and loves those who cheerfully give. When you are generous, you fill the earth with the glory of God.

Generosity is the "krypton" of leadership. The element krypton, appearing on the periodic chart of elements is, basically, an inert chemical. But, when used in fluorescent bulbs, krypton makes the light whiter and brighter. When used in laser lights, krypton makes them more powerful and precise. Like the element krypton, rich generosity lights up leadership—leadership that separates and distinguishes great leaders from good leaders. Great leaders excel in the transformative, wasteful generosity of their time, talent, and treasure.

First, leaders are generous with their time. Sarah is a nurse manager in a 208-bed hospital. She is a deeply dedicated, busy, and caring medical practitioner. She has hundreds of people contacts each day with her patients, family members of patients, nursing staff, physicians, social workers, and numerous other hospital personnel. She completes mountains of paperwork each day, charts patients' needs and progress, monitors infection control, and assures that all state and federal healthcare standards are maintained and exceeded.

Yet, Sarah always has time for people. For example, at least once each week, Sarah spends time, one-on-one, with each member of her nursing team. She may catch them in the hallway, in the linen closet, at the nursing station, or in the lunch room. There she conducts her "3x5 Card Performance Appraisal." In reality, there is no 3x5 card, and it's not a formal performance appraisal. Individually, privately, and informally she asks three questions: 1) "What have you done this week that you are particularly proud of?" 2) "What have you done this week, that if you had it to do all over again, you would do differently?" 3) "In what area of your work do you need my help?" Yes, Sarah views this activity as an important part of her leadership role at the hospital. Yes, the performance of the healthcare staff improves each week. Most importantly, the staff respects (even reveres) Sarah, because, as they put it, "She spends *time* with me." Leaders, like Sarah, are gloriously generous with their time.

Leaders are generous with their talent. Leaders have taken the time to inventory and assess their own created attributes (the topic of this book), personality traits, spiritual gifts, passions, skills, abilities, vision, and mission. They then intentionally focus these assets in places of work and service that make a difference for others. Sarah has the gift of mercy. She actively focuses this asset on her patients at the hospital, volunteers this talent working with the homeless in her community, and is an enthusiastic and energetic participant in the mercy ministries of her church. The focused exercise of this talent is transforming—making a positive difference in the lives of hundreds of people throughout her community. Leaders, like Sarah, are generous with their talent.

Finally, leaders are generous with their treasure, that is, their money and possessions. Leaders fully understand that God created everything, and retains ownership of everything. Everything they "possess" is actually owned by God. Leaders understand that if God owns everything, then what they "own" has only been entrusted to them by God. Leaders simply view themselves as "managers" or "stewards"—not "owners." As a steward of God's money, then, leaders realize that they must manage money and possessions according to God's (the Owner's) standards and guidelines. Stewardship of God's money involves much more than discreetly dropping a dollar bill into the collection plate on Sunday—much more than giving 10% to the church. Generosity is the stewardship of everything God has entrusted—including the 90% that remains after the tithe. The stewardship of money is the generous, lavish, exuberant, even wasteful, generosity of God's money.

Sarah is generous with money. She tithes to her church, gives extra money for special projects and ministries, and supports teens that take short-term mission trips. She delights in purchasing special gifts for her friends, neighbors, and employees. Because Sarah has the gift of mercy, her heart goes out to the homeless—some of whom approach her on the street asking for money so they can "buy something to eat." She always gives some money to each person. Some think Sarah is wasteful—that these people are nothing but "professional panhandlers." But Sarah never questions their "need" or the motive for asking. She is "wastefully generous" with those who have less.

## The Mark of Generous Leadership

Many well-known leaders have addressed this matter of the generosity of money. The well-known American evangelist, Billy Graham, noted the important relationship between one's spiritual health and their checkbook, "Give me five minutes with a person's checkbook, and I will tell you where their heart is." Colonel

Sanders (1890—1980), the founder of KFC, quipped, "There's no need to be the richest man in the cemetery." The New York author, Christian Bovee (1820—1904) wisely noted, "Examples are few of men ruined by giving." Anne Frank (1929—1945), the young Jewish girl who wrote a diary while hiding with her family and friends in Amsterdam during the German occupation of the Netherlands during World War II, observed, "No one has ever become poor by giving." Author Charles H. Burr put it this way, "Getters generally don't get happiness; givers get it." Bishop Fulton J. Sheen (1895—1979), renowned Roman Catholic bishop and author, put a sobering understanding to generosity, "Never measure your generosity by what you give but rather by what you have left." S. Truett Cathy, philanthropist and founder of Chick-fil-A Restaurants, was very comfortable about having money but warned, "It's okay to have wealth. But keep it in your hand, not in your heart."

The mark of effective leadership is to give, and give, then give even more of your time, talent, and treasure. Like God, be gloriously and wastefully generous. Like the greedy king in *The Quiltmaker's Gift*, you will never be as happy as when you are giving away your money, your possessions, your time, and your talents. In the words of John Wesley (1703—1791), the founder of Methodism, "Earn as much as you can. Save as much as you can. Invest as much as your can. Give as much as you can."

## Cultivating Generous Leadership

It is crucial that you begin, today, to reclaim, cultivate, and steward this important leadership attribute. Begin by completing the "Personal Reflection" exercise that follows. Take time to thoughtfully and intentionally reflect on each question before recording your responses. Invest quality time in responding to each question. Then complete the "Cultivating Your Created Leadership

Capacity." This exercise will help you think through how best to apply gloriously generous leadership in each one of your major life roles and spheres of influence. Remember, you are generous. As a leader you possess the created capacity and responsibility to be generous as God is generous, dispensing the sacrificial generosity of God to those around you by being supremely and wastefully generous with your time, talent, and treasure.

You are generous. You are a leader. This is the truth about leadership. This is the *Genesis Principle of Leadership*.

# Personal Reflection

### *Leaders are Generous*

- Leadership is reclaiming and cultivating your God-given, created attributes. What specific action steps will you take to develop this leadership trait: Generous?

- What does it mean that God is generous?

- List three ways in which God has been generous to you:

- List some specific actions you can take to be generous to others:

- Which action will you implement this week?

- To whom?

- What result(s) do you expect from taking this action?

- Take a few moments—now—to pray about this action.

- In what way(s) could you help someone in your family, workplace, or community claim and cultivate this leadership attribute in his life?

- Cultivate this created leadership trait by completing the "Cultivating Your Leadership Attributes" exercise on the next page.

## Cultivating Your Created Leadership Capacity

Leadership is the lifelong pursuit of claiming and cultivating your God-created attributes.

1. 1) Select a Life Role (e.g. Leader, Spouse, Parent, Worker, Neighbor, etc.).
2. 2) List the key Duties and Responsibilities of that Life Role.
3. 3) Then design and list specific Action Steps that will enable you to steward this leadership attribute.

## Cultivating Generous Leadership

As a leader you possess the created capacity and responsibility to be generous as God is generous, dispensing the sacrificial generosity of God to those around you by being supremely and wastefully generous with your time, talent, and treasure.

## Life Role:

_____

| Duties/Responsibilities: | Leadership is Action: |
|---|---|
| 1. | |
| 2. | |
| 3. | |
| 4. | |
| 5. | |
| 6. | |
| 7. | |

*What you do with what you know is what
Christian knowing is all about.* (Os Guinness)

# The Essential Purpose of the Human Enterprise

"...the restoration within us of the long-lost image of God."

John Amos Comenius (1592–1670)[74]

## Finding Your Leadership Voice

Pastor John was deeply concerned about the illiteracy of the children in his parish. His church served a rural, agricultural area. Life in this farming country was demanding. The days were long. Everyone worked hard from sunup to sundown. Work on the family farms required the help of everyone—particularly the children. As soon as they were able to walk, the children worked alongside their parents. Children were essential to the success of the family farm. Consequently, there was no time for learning reading, writing, and arithmetic. Going to school was a luxury only the noble and wealthy people in the surrounding villages could enjoy.

Nevertheless, Pastor John convinced the parishioners in his church to allow their children to stay for a few hours following the Sunday worship service so that he could teach them reading, writing, arithmetic, and Latin. Pastor John called this innovative program, "Sunday School." As far as I can discern, this may be the first record of "Sunday School" in church history. Curiously, though, his "Sunday School" was for the purpose of providing a well-rounded education to the boys and girls in the parish.

Known today as the "Father of Pedagogy," Pastor John Amos Comenius (1592–1670) pioneered several modern educational methodologies at his "Sunday School" in Moravia (now known as the Czech Republic). He was the first to use pictures in his textbooks; the first to include women in his school; and, the first to believe that learning was a cradle-to-the-grave process. He wrote over 150 books (some of his Latin textbooks are still in use today); believed that learning, spiritual maturity, and emotional growth were intricately woven together; documented the distinctive learning styles of children of varying ages; and, formulated an educational model based upon the developmental growth of children (which he named "pedagogy"—the art and science of teaching children). There is evidence that he turned down an offer to become the first president of Harvard University.

John Amos Comenius was among the first to call for a universal education. Since all people of both sexes are equal partakers of the image of God and share in His grace equally, then both must be equal partakers of education and training, which seeks the restoration within us of the long-lost image of God. As Comenius argued:

> They (females) are endowed with equal sharpness of mind and capacity for knowledge...and are able to attain the highest positions since they have often been called by

God Himself to rule over nations, to give sound advice to kings and princes...even to the office of prophesying and inveighing against priests and bishops.

*The Great Didactic, IX: 5*

John Amos Comenius was also the first to believe that learning, spiritual growth, and mental/emotional development was intricately woven together. He held a classical, traditional, biblical view of the person believing that the essential purpose of education was to enable every child to be fully conformed to the image of God. "The restoration within us of the long-forgotten image of God" was the driving vision for his "Sunday School." Comenius believed that the essential purpose of the human enterprise—in every sphere of life—was rooted in man's call to fill the earth with the glory of God through the restored created attributes of God. Once restored, we would be able to fully participate in God's divine redemptive purpose, which ultimately leads to the restoration and liberation of the entire fallen creation. This notion resonates with the Apostle Paul's words to the church at Rome:

> For the creation was subjected to futility, not willingly, but because of him who subjected it, in hope that the creation itself will be set free from its bondage to decay and obtain the freedom of the glory of the children of God.
>
> Romans 8:20–21 (ESV)

Comenius was convinced that authentic human living begins with the imitation of God. He approached all of life guided by a biblical view of personhood. Life was to be a "garden of delight" where we, as "gardeners," are to "water God's plants," enabling each person to "find his voice." In this way, each and every person becomes "a garden of delight for his God." Toward this end, Comenius emphasized bringing faith and reason together into what he called "harmonic interrelation." By this, he meant that faith and reason are to compliment each other in such a way as to teach all things to all men from all points of view. Such an approach ultimately promotes the rediscovery and restoration of the long-lost attributes (image) of God.

## Comenius Had It Right!

The redemption of all men and women and boys and girls *is* for one purpose: to fill the earth again with the glory of God through the restored attributes of God within each and every person. The central purpose of the church, the family, education, and, particularly leadership is to take mankind back to its first and original condition—the good creation. Convinced of the importance of this task, pastors must focus their preaching, teaching, and shepherding toward enabling every member of their congregations to reclaim and cultivate the long-lost attributes of God. Parents must reorder their priorities toward the cultivation of the created attributes in their children. Educators must recapture a high, traditional, biblical view of their students and radically alter their pedagogical approaches to training and developing children. Employers must change their low, mechanistic views of the worker enabling their employees to recapture a high and holy view of work and personhood. As this occurs, everyone will delight in God's image and become His garden of delight—people will delight in God—God will delight in His image bearers—and the earth will be filled with God's glory. It will fulfill Comenius' dream who prayed:

Do thou, everlasting wisdom, who dost play in this world and whose delight is in the sons of men, ensure that we in turn may now find delight in thee. Discover more fully unto us ways and means to better understanding of thy play and to more eager pursuance of it with one another until we ourselves finally play in thy company more effectively to give increasing pleasure unto thee, who art our everlasting delight! Amen!

## The Central Purpose of Leadership

Seeking the restoration of the long-forgotten image of God is the essential purpose of leadership. When grasped, this goal establishes a leadership paradigm that is biblically informed, yet dynamically effective in bringing together the theological, philosophical, and pragmatic dimensions of leadership. The renewal of the long-forgotten image of God in us is the central purpose and organizing principle of leadership. Every organization needs all the good managers it can find. I would suggest that finding and developing managers (in other words, people who know how to do things right) is not all that difficult. Seldom, if ever, do organizations collapse because there are not enough good managers. Organizations collapse for the lack of leaders. In spite of the glut of leadership literature and seminars, organizations continue to collapse because there are simply not enough people who lead. Most professional development seminars and books are ineffective because they continue to miss the mark regarding this essential purpose of leadership.

The key to developing effective leaders is helping people restore the long-forgotten image of God within them. Leaders are to help others reclaim and steward the created attributes of God within those they lead. Leaders must become more conscious of men and women as being made in the image of God. Therefore, they possess the God-created, God-given attributes. Leaders must see that people are not driven by the evolutionary forces of genetics or the developmental press of the environment. People are not in the process of perceiving, behaving, or becoming a fully functioning self, nor are they in a lifelong pursuit of self-actualization. Rather, leadership and the development of leaders must be specifically directed at enabling each person to reclaim (structurally) the long-forgotten attributes of God and to cultivate (functionally) each created leadership attribute.

## The Leadership Mandate

In this sense, leaders must lead everyone in the process of discovering that we are all leaders. As the created attributes are reclaimed and cultivated, everyone must lead in their particular spheres of influence. People must assume leadership within their families, churches, places of employment, and communities. They must use their gifts, talents, and abilities to affect positive and intentional change for the benefit of themselves and others. Therefore, leadership must enable each person to reclaim the characteristics of God given to him as a bearer of God's image. Leadership must help others fulfill their mandate to reflect and represent the image of God. Leadership must help every person do that which God put them on earth to do: fill the earth with His glory. This is leadership in its ultimate, created, eternal, and fullest sense. Show me a person who is actively reclaiming and cultivating their created attributes (i.e. active and purposeful, rational, creative, exercise dominion, moral, relational, free and responsible, loving, merciful, faithful, interdependent, and generous), and I will show you a true leader.

Leaders are not born! Leaders are not made! Leaders are created! Each one of us has been created with the full capacity for this one essential purpose of the human enterprise—to restore within yourself and within each other the long-forgotten image of God so that we can fill the earth with the glory of God. You were created for this purpose.

You were created to lead!

You have the created capacity for leadership!

This is the truth about leadership!

This is the *Genesis Principle of Leadership!*

Now go out and lead!

# Personal Reflection

*The Essential Purpose of the Human Enterprise*

- Leadership is reclaiming and cultivating your God-given, created attributes. As a leader what specific action steps will you take to assist others restore within them the long-lost image of God?

- What does it mean that you are created in the image of God?

- If you are a pastor or Sunday school teacher, how will you design your sermon or Sunday school lesson to help others reclaim and cultivate the created attributes in your children?

- As a parent, list three things you can do today to help restore the long-lost attributes of God in your children's lives.

- If you are school teacher, what learning activities can you incorporate into today's lesson plans that will enable your students to reflect the image of God in their lives?

- If you are an employer, manager, or supervisor, what new approaches to leadership will enable your employees to steward their own created attributes?

- What result(s) do you expect from taking these actions?

- Take a few moments—now—to pray about your "plan of action."

# Endnotes

1. Covey, Stephen R., *Seven Habits of Highly Effective People: Powerful Lessons in Personal Change*, 15th Anniversary Edition, New York, New York, Simon and Schuster, 2004.

2. Covey, Stephen R., *The 8th Habit: From Effectiveness to Greatness*, Tampa, FL, Free Press 2004.

3. Blank, Warren, *The 9 Natural Laws of Leadership*, New York, American Management Association, 1995.

4. Pitino, Rick and Reynolds, Bill, *Lead to Succeed: Ten Traits of Great Leadership in Business and Life*, Louisville, KY, Broadway Books, 2000.

5. Brown, W. Stephen, *13 Fatal Errors Managers Make and How You Can Avoid Them*, Berkley, Mass Market Paperback, 1995.

6. Maxwell, John C., *The 17 Indispensable Laws of Teamwork: Embrace Them and Empower Your Team*, Nashville, TN, Thomas Nelson Publishers, 2003.

7. Maxwell, John C., *The 21 Indispensable Qualities of a Leader: Become the Person Others Will Want to Follow*, Nashville, TN,

Thomas Nelson Publishers, 1999.

8. Benton, D. A., *How to Think Like a CEO: The 22 Vital Traits You Need to Be the Person at the Top*, Lebanon, IN, Little Brown and Company, 1999.

9. Elffers, Joost and Greene, Robert, New York, *The 48 Laws of Power*, Penguin USA, 2000.

10. Sennewald, Charles A., *Jackass Management*, Sugar Land, Texas, Sennewald-Vellani Publishing Co., Date Unknown.

11. Horowitz, Adam, Jacobson, David, Lasswell, Mark, and Thomas, Owen, "The 101 Dumbest Moments in Business: 2005's Shenanigans, Skullduggery and Just Plain Stupidity," Magazine, *CNNMoney.com*, February, 2006.

12. Blank, Warren, *The 108 Skills of Natural Born Leaders*, New York, American Management Association, 2001.

13. Kaser, Joyce, Mundry, Susan, Stiles, Katherine E., and Louchs-Horsley, Susan, *Leading Every Day: 124 Actions for Effective Leadership*, Thousand Oaks, CA, Corwin Press, Inc, 2002.

14. Baldoni, John, *180 Ways to Walk the Leadership Talk: The How to Handbook for Leaders at All Levels*, Walk the Talk Publishing, 2000.

15. *Webster's Ninth New Collegiate Dictionary*, Merriam-Webster Inc. Publishers, Springfield, Massachusetts, 1987.

16. Kellerman, Barbara "Required Reading," *Harvard Business Review*, December 2001, 79 (11) 15–24.

17. Plato, *The Republic*, Hackett Publishing Company, 2nd edition, Indianapolis, 1992.

18. Plato, *The Republic,* Hackett Publishing Company, 2nd edition, Indianapolis, 1992.

19. Cohen, David, "Behaviorism," *The Oxford Companion to the Mind,* Richard L. Gregory, ed., New York, Oxford University Press, 1987, p. 71.

20. Smith, C. U. M., *The Brain,* New York, Capricorn Books, 1972, p. 35.

21. Brooks, David, "The Organization Kid," *The Atlantic Monthly,* April, 2001, p. 8.

22. Ridley, Matt, "What Makes You Who You Are," *Time Magazine,* June 2, 2004, p. 54–63.

23. Evans, C. Stephen, *Preserving the Person: A Look at the Human Sciences,* Grand Rapids, MI, Baker Book House, 1977, p. 14.

24. Hoekema, Anthony A., *Created in God's Image,* Grand Rapids, MI, William B. Eerdmans Publishing Company, 1986, p.1.

25. Hoekema, Anthony A., *Created in God's Image,* Grand Rapids, MI, William B. Eerdmans Publishing Company, 1986, p.1.

26. Calvin, John, *Commentary on Corinthians,* Christian Class Ethereal Library, Grand Rapids, 1999, 15:49

27. Guiness, Os, *The Calling: Finding and Fulfilling The Central Purpose of Your Life,* Nashville, TN, Word Publishing, 1998, p. 7.

28. Pinkola-Estes, Clarissa, *Women Who Run With the Wolves,* Ballantine Books, New York, 1992.

29. Havel, Vaclav, "Summer Meditations," *Sunrise Magazine,* April/May, 1992.

30. Scriven, Michael and Paul, Richard, "Defining Critical Thinking: A Draft Statement," *The National Council for Excellence in Critical Thinking.* Date Unknown.

31. Havel, Vaclav, "Summer Meditations," *Sunrise Magazine,* April/May, 1992.

32. Guinness, Os, Chapel Talk, Covenant College, 2001.

33. Sumner, William Graham, *Folkways,* 1906, pp. 632–633.

34. Michalko, Michael, *Cracking Creativity: The Secrets of Creative Genius,* Berkley, CA, Ten Speed Press, 2001.

35. Michalko, Michael, *Cracking Creativity: The Secrets of Creative Genius,* Berkley, CA, Ten Speed Press, 2001.

36. Michalko, Michael, *Cracking Creativity: The Secrets of Creative Genius,* Berkley, CA, Ten Speed Press, 2001

37. Michalko, Michael, *Thinkpad: A Brainstorming Card Deck,* Berkley, CA, Ten Speed Press, 1994.

38. Michalko, Michael, *Tinkertoys: A Handbook of Business Creativity,* Berkley, CA, Ten Speed Press, 1991.

39. Spurgeon, C. H., Quoted in *The Attributes of God* by A. W. Pink, PBM Publications, Texas, 2005.

40. King, Martin Luther, A Knock at Midnight: Inspiration from the Great Sermons of Reverend Martin Luther King, Jr., Hachette Audio, May, 1998.

41. http://www.thecityreview.com/

42. Pope Paul VI, *Gaudium et Spes,* n.16, 1965.

43. Rousseau, Jean Jacques, *Profession of Faith of a Savoyard Vicar*, The Harvard Classics, 1909–1914.

44. Huntsman, Jon M., *Winners Never Cheat*, Wharton School Publishing, NJ, 2005, p. 176.

45. Putnam, Robert, *Bowling Alone: The Collapse and Revival of American Community*. Simon and Schuster, 2000, New York.

46. Alexis de Tocqueville, *Democracy in America*, ed. J. P. Mater, Anchor, 1969, New York, p. 513–517

47. Howe, Leroy, *The Image of God: A Theology for Pastoral Care and Counseling*. Nashville, Abingdon, 1995, p. 15.

48. *The Shorter Catechism*, The Committee for Christian Education and Publications, Presbyterian Church in America, Lawrenceville, Georgia, 3rd Edition. p. 3.

49. Henry, Matthew, Matthew Henry's Commentary on the Whole Bible, Vol. 5, Matthew to John, MacDonald Publishing Company, McLean, Virginia, 1721, p. 324–326.

50. Bennis, Warren and Nanus, Burt, *Leaders*, New York, Harper and Row, 1985, p. 76.

51. *The Catechism of the Catholic Church*, Second Edition, 1992.

52. Apisdorf, Rabbi Shimon, "Freedom and Responsibility," AISH.com, retrieved from the internet on August 10, 2006.

53. Friesen, Garry, *Decision Making and the Will of God*, Multnomah Press, Portland, OR, 1980.

54. www.SeattleTimes.newsource.com

55. www.SeattleTimes.newsource.com

56. Fenton, Bruce, Fenton Report: *Wealth Management Magazine*, www.fentonreport.com, March 28, 2005.

57. Loving, Christopher J., *Loving Leadership: Rekindling the Human Spirit to Business, Relationships, and Life*, Listen and Live Audio, Inc. www.audible.com, 1996.

58. Watson, Thomas, *Body of Divinity Contained in Sermons Upon the Assembly's Catechism*, Westminster Shorter Catechism Project, http://www.bpc.org/resources/watson/wsc_wa_049-052_b.html.

59. Blue Letter Bible: http://www.blueletterbible.org/

60. Shakespeare, William, *The Merchant of Venice*, 1597?

61. Goldman, William, *The Princess Bride*, Movie, 1987.

62. Box, Sir Arnold, "Farewell, My Youth," 1943, p. 17.

63. Prynne, William, *Histriomastix*, 1622.

64. LaCugna, Catherine Mowry, *God for Us, The Trinity and Christian Life*, New York, NY, Harper Collins Publishing, 1992, p. 271.

65. Ferguson, Sinclair, *The Holy Spirit*, Intervarsity Press, Downers Grove, IL, 1996, p. 188. Johnson, Spencer and Blanchard, Kenneth H., *One-Minute Manager*, HarperCollins Business, New York, 2000.

66. Damick, Andrew Stephen, "Perichoresis," 2004.

67. Blanchard, Kenneth and Spencer, Johnson, *The One Minute Manager*, William Morrow, Publisher, 1982.

68. Kossoff, Leslie, *Executive Thinking: The Dream, The Vision, The*

*Mission Achieved*, Davies-Black Publishing, 1999.

69. Kotter, John. P., *Leading Change*, Harvard Business School Press, 1996.

70. Clawson, James, *Level Three Leadership: Getting Below the Surface*, Pearson/Prentice Hall, 2006, 2003, 1999.

71. Clawson, James, *Level Three Leadership: Getting Below the Surface*, Pearson/Prentice Hall, 2006, 2003, 1999, p.

72. Brumbeau, Jeff and De Marcken, Gail, *The Quiltmaker's Gift*, Scholastic Press, 2001.

73. MacDonald, George, *The Diary of an Old Man: 366 Writings for Devotional Reflection*, Augsburg Fortress Publishers, Minneapolis, 1994.

74. Comenius, John Amos Comenius, *The Great Didactic*, vol. xvi: 2.